CW00539296

FORENSIC ASPECTS OF
DISSOCIATIVE IDENTITY DISORDER

Other titles in the
Forensic Psychotherapy Monograph Series

FORENSIC ASPECTS OF DISSOCIATIVE IDENTITY DISORDER

Edited by
Adah Sachs & Graeme Galton

Forensic Psychotherapy Monograph Series

Series Editor
Brett Kahr

Honorary Consultant
Estela Welldon

KARNAC

First published in 2008 by
Karnac Books
118 Finchley Road
London NW3 5HT

Arrangement copyright © 2008 by Adah Sachs & Graeme Galton; Introduction
& chapter 10 copyright © 2008 by Adah Sachs; chapter 1 copyright © 2008
by Joan Coleman; chapter 2 copyright © 2008 by Chris Healey; chapter 3
copyright © 2008 by Thorsten Becker, Wanda Karriker, Bettina Overkamp, &
Carol Rutz; chapter 4 copyright © 2008 by "Aahbee"; chapter 5 copyright ©
2008 by Sue Cross & "Louise"; chapter 6 copyright © 2008 by James Farmer,
Warwick Middleton, & John Devereux; chapters 7 & 14 copyright © 2008
by Valerie Sinason; chapter 8 copyright © 2008 by Phil Mollon; chapter 9
copyright © 2008 by Graeme Galton; chapter 11 copyright © 2008 by Alison
Anderson; chapter 12 copyright © 2008 by John Silverstone; chapter 13
copyright © 2008 by Sue Cook; chapter 15 copyright © 2008 by Ellen P. Lacter

The rights of the editor and contributors to be identified as the authors of this
work have been asserted in accordance with §§ 77 and 78 of the Copyright
Design and Patents Act 1988.

All rights reserved. No part of this publication may be reproduced, stored in
a retrieval system, or transmitted, in any form or by any means, electronic,
mechanical, photocopying, recording, or otherwise, without the prior written
permission of the publisher.

British Library Cataloguing in Publication Data

A C.I.P. for this book is available from the British Library

ISBN: 978-1-85575-596-3

Edited, designed, and produced by Communication Crafts

Printed in Great Britain

www.karnacbooks.com

To the memory of Helen

Adah Sachs

CONTENTS

ACKNOWLEDGEMENTS

I would like to express my gratitude to Valerie Sinason, my inspirational teacher, guide, and friend; to Brett Kahr, who thought I could write this book; to Graeme Galton, who joined me when I nearly gave up, and who made this book happen; to my patients, who taught me about DID, and about courage and commitment; and to my family, who held me through it all.

Adah Sachs

My warmest thanks to my valued colleagues and friends, Valerie Sinason and Adah Sachs, with whom I am privileged to work. My gratitude to all the talented and thoughtful contributors who generously responded to our invitation to write for this book. As ever, my most important teachers have been my patients, and I thank them for putting their trust in me.

Graeme Galton

SERIES FOREWORD

Brett Kahr

Centre for Child Mental Health, London
and
The Winnicott Clinic of Psychotherapy, London

Throughout most of human history, our ancestors have done rather poorly when dealing with acts of violence. To cite but one of many shocking examples, let us perhaps recall a case from 1801, of an English boy aged only 13, who was executed by hanging on the gallows at Tyburn. What was his crime? It seems that he had been condemned to die for having stolen a spoon (Westwick, 1940).

In most cases, our predecessors have either *ignored* murderousness and aggression, as in the case of Graeco–Roman infanticide, which occurred so regularly in the ancient world that it acquired an almost normative status (deMause, 1974; Kahr, 1994); or they have *punished* murderousness and destruction with retaliatory sadism, a form of unconscious identification with the aggressor. Any history of criminology will readily reveal the cruel punishments inflicted upon prisoners throughout the ages, ranging from beatings and stockades, to more severe forms of torture, culminating in eviscerations, beheadings, or lynchings.

Only during the last one hundred years have we begun to develop the capacity to respond more intelligently and more humanely to acts of dangerousness and destruction. Since the advent of psychoanalysis

xiii

and psychoanalytic psychotherapy, we now have access to a much deeper understanding both of the aetiology of aggressive acts and of their treatment; and nowadays we need no longer ignore criminals or abuse them—instead, we can provide compassion and containment, as well as conduct research that can help to prevent future acts of violence.

The modern discipline of forensic psychotherapy, which can be defined, quite simply, as the use of psychoanalytically orientated "talking therapy" to treat violent, offender patients, stems directly from the work of Sigmund Freud. Almost one hundred years ago, at a meeting of the Vienna Psycho-Analytical Society, held on 6 February 1907, Sigmund Freud anticipated the clarion call of contemporary forensic psychotherapists when he bemoaned the often horrible treatment of mentally ill offenders, in a discussion on the psychology of vagrancy. According to Otto Rank, Freud's secretary at the time, the founder of psychoanalysis expressed his sorrow at the "nonsensical treatment of these people in prisons" (quoted in Nunberg & Federn, 1962, p. 108).

Many of the early psychoanalysts preoccupied themselves with forensic topics. Hanns Sachs, himself a trained lawyer, and Marie Bonaparte, the French princess who wrote about the cruelty of war, each spoke fiercely against capital punishment. Sachs, one of the first members of Freud's secret committee, regarded the death penalty for offenders as an example of group sadism (Moellenhoff, 1966). Bonaparte, who had studied various murderers throughout her career, had actually lobbied politicians in America to free the convicted killer Caryl Chessman, during his sentence on Death Row at the California State Prison in San Quentin, albeit unsuccessfully (Bertin, 1982).

Melanie Klein concluded her first book, the landmark text *Die Psychoanalyse des Kindes* [*The Psycho-Analysis of Children*], with resounding passion about the problem of violence in our culture. Mrs Klein noted that acts of criminality invariably stem from disturbances in childhood, and that if young people could receive access to psychoanalytic treatment at any early age, then much cruelty could be prevented in later years. Klein expressed the hope that: "If every child who shows disturbances that are at all severe were to be analysed in good time, a great number of these people who later end up in prisons or lunatic asylums, or who go completely to pieces, would be saved from such a fate and be able to develop a normal life" (1932, p. 374).

Shortly after the publication of Klein's transformative book, Atwell Westwick, a Judge of the Superior Court of Santa Barbara, California, published a little-known though highly inspiring article, "Criminology and Psychoanalysis" (1940), in the *Psychoanalytic Quarterly*. Westwick may well be the first judge to commit himself in print to the value of psychoanalysis in the study of criminality, arguing that punishment of the forensic patient remains, in fact, a sheer waste of time. With foresight, Judge Westwick queried, "Can we not, in our well nigh hopeless and overwhelming struggle with the problems of delinquency and crime, profit by medical experience with the problems of health and disease? Will we not, eventually, terminate the senseless policy of sitting idly by until misbehavior occurs, often with irreparable damage, then dumping the delinquent into the juvenile court or reformatory and dumping the criminal into prison?" (p. 281). Westwick noted that we should, instead, train judges, probation officers, social workers, as well as teachers and parents, in the precepts of psychoanalysis, in order to arrive at a more sensitive, non-punitive understanding of the nature of criminality. He opined: "When we shall have succeeded in committing society to such a program, when we see it launched definitely upon the venture, as in time it surely will be—then shall we have erected an appropriate memorial to Sigmund Freud" (p. 281).

In more recent years, the field of forensic psychotherapy has become increasingly well constellated. Building upon the pioneering contributions of such psychoanalysts and psychotherapists as Edward Glover, Grace Pailthorpe, Melitta Schmideberg, and more recently Murray Cox, Mervin Glasser, Ismond Rosen, Estela Welldon, and others too numerous to mention, forensic psychotherapy has now become an increasingly formalized discipline that can be dated to the inauguration of the International Association for Forensic Psychotherapy and to the first annual conference, held at St. Bartholomew's Hospital in London in 1991. The profession now boasts a more robust foundation, with training courses developing in the United Kingdom and beyond. Since the inauguration of the Diploma in Forensic Psychotherapy (and subsequently the Diploma in Forensic Psychotherapeutic Studies), under the auspices of the British Postgraduate Medical Federation of the University of London in association with the Portman Clinic, students can now seek further instruction in the psychodynamic treatment of patients who act out in a dangerous and illegal manner.

The volumes in this series of books will aim to provide both practical advice and theoretical stimulation for introductory students and for senior practitioners alike. In the Karnac Books Forensic Psychotherapy Monograph Series, we will endeavour to produce a regular stream of high-quality titles, written by leading members of the profession, who will share their expertise in a concise and practice-orientated fashion. We trust that such a collection of books will help to consolidate the knowledge and experience that we have already acquired and will also provide new directions for the upcoming decades of the new century. In this way, we shall hope to plant the seeds for a more rigorous, sturdy, and wide-reaching profession of forensic psychotherapy.

As the new millennium begins to unfold, we now have an opportunity for psychotherapeutically orientated forensic mental health professionals to work in close conjunction with child psychologists and with infant mental health specialists so that the problems of violence can be tackled both preventatively and retrospectively. With the growth of the field of forensic psychotherapy, we at last have reason to be hopeful that serious criminality can be forestalled and perhaps, one day, even eradicated.

References

Bertin, C. (1982). *La Dernière Bonaparte*. Paris: Librairie Académique Perrin.

deMause, L. (1974). The evolution of childhood. In: Lloyd deMause (Ed.), *The History of Childhood* (pp. 1–73). New York: Psychohistory Press.

Kahr, B. (1994). The historical foundations of ritual abuse: an excavation of ancient infanticide. In: Valerie Sinason (Ed.), *Treating Survivors of Satanist Abuse* (pp. 45–56). London: Routledge.

Klein, M. (1932). *The Psycho-Analysis of Children*, trans. Alix Strachey. London: Hogarth Press and The Institute of Psycho-Analysis. [First published as *Die Psychoanalyse des Kindes*. Vienna: Internationaler Psychoanalytischer Verlag.]

Moellenhoff, F. (1966). Hanns Sachs, 1881–1947: the creative unconscious. In: F. Alexander, S. Eisenstein, & M. Grotjahn (Eds.), *Psychoanalytic Pioneers* (pp. 180–199). New York: Basic Books.

Nunberg, H., & Federn, E. (Eds.) (1962). *Minutes of the Vienna Psychoanalytic Society. Volume I: 1906–1908*, trans. Margarethe Nunberg. New York: International Universities Press.

Westwick, A. (1940). Criminology and Psychoanalysis. *Psychoanalytic Quarterly*, 9: 269–282.

"Aahbee" is a medical doctor, married for 25 years, with three children. She has worked part-time in the National Health Service in the United Kingdom for over 20 years. She has also been an accredited counsellor. For several years, she served as a Chair of School Governors. She now works for charitable trusts supporting adult survivors of childhood neglect, trauma, and abuse. She was diagnosed with dissociative identity disorder four years ago, during a severe depressive episode, and is on a therapy-based journey of recovery.

Alison Anderson is a general practitioner working in the National Health Service in Surrey. Her special interests are paediatrics and mental health. She is married and has four children.

Thorsten Becker is a social worker and freelance supervisor in Germany. In his work as a cult counsellor, he has served as case consultant in several suspected cult-related investigations in Europe. In 1994, he received the "German Child Protection Award" for his team's work with ritually abused children.

Joan Coleman graduated in medicine in 1956, and worked as a general practitioner in the National Health Service in the United Kingdom. She specialized in psychiatry, gaining her MRCPsych in 1975. She worked for twenty-five years in a psychiatric hospital in Surrey. She treated both acute and chronic psychiatric patients, including those with physical, as well as psychiatric, disorders. During that time she developed a special interest in the subject of ritual abuse and dissociative identity disorder. She retired from NHS work in 1994. She is a founder member and membership coordinator of RAINS (Ritual Abuse Information Network and Support).

Sue Cook is a trained Christian counsellor. She works in private practice, increasingly specializing in complex trauma, attachment, and dissociation. She is trained in the treatment of trauma and developmental injury using the sensorimotor psychotherapy approach. She also works closely with the Clinic for Dissociative Studies in London. She lives in Surrey with her husband and has three grown-up children.

Sue Cross is a qualified pharmacist, a counsellor and supervisor in private practice in Surrey. In the past few years, she has worked primarily in the field of trauma and dissociation and has several clients with dissociative identity disorder. She is a registered counsellor with Deep Release, a Christian counselling and training organization based in Essex, and she is involved in training, research, and course development on trauma and dissociation.

John Devereux is Professor of Common Law at the T.C. Beirne School of Law, University of Queensland, Australia. He has degrees in Arts and Law from the University of Queensland, and a Doctorate of Philosophy from Oxford University; the latter was gained while he was a Rhodes Scholar. He has served as a Law Reform Commissioner for Queensland. He is an Honorary Fellow of the Australian College of Legal Medicine and is a Barrister of the Supreme Court of Queensland.

James Farmer began working with the Public Defender's Office in Brisbane, Australia, as a para-legal in 1979, when he began his studies in law. After that office was amalgamated with the Legal

Aid Office in 1990, he was appointed as a trial counsel. One of his first cases involved a defence of unsoundness of mind based on a diagnosis of multiple personality disorder. He has appeared in trials in both Superior Court jurisdictions in Queensland, in appeals, and in the Mental Health Court (which determines the question of unsoundness of mind) for patients charged with indictable offences. He is presently undertaking postgraduate studies at the University of Queensland. His thesis topic deals with the criminal responsibility of dissociative identity disorder sufferers.

Graeme Galton was born in Australia and lives in London. He is a psychoanalytic psychotherapist in the National Health Service and in private practice. He is a consultant psychotherapist at the Clinic for Dissociative Studies, a small specialist outpatient mental health service for people suffering from severe trauma and dissociation. He also works at the Parkside Clinic in London, working with individuals and groups in an NHS outpatient psychotherapy service. He is a registered member of the Centre for Attachment-Based Psychoanalytic Psychotherapy, where he is a training supervisor and teaches on the clinical training programme. He is also a visiting tutor at the School of Psychotherapy and Counselling Psychology, Regent's College, London. He edited the book *Touch Papers: Dialogues on Touch in the Psychoanalytic Space* (2006).

Chris Healey joined Hampshire Constabulary in 1972, and then the Criminal Investigation Department (CID) in 1979 in Portsmouth. During his career in the CID he served in various posts in local crime units, local intelligence, Special Branch, and Scientific Services. During the postings in the Scientific Services he was the Head of Fingerprints, and was seconded to Her Majesties Inspector of Constabulary to inspect and report on the Scientific Services, which culminated in the report, *Under the Microscope*. He was the Head of CID in Portsmouth for several years and retired in 2003.

Wanda Karriker is a retired psychologist in the United States. She has been interviewed on Court TV as an expert on ritual abuse. She has written about the after-effects of extreme child abuse and the resilience of the human spirit in her novel, *Morning, Come Quickly*.

Ellen P. Lacter is a Licensed Clinical Psychologist, Registered Play Therapist and Supervisor, and Licensed Marriage and Family Therapist. She is Academic Coordinator of the Play Therapy Certificate programme at the University of California, San Diego Extension. She specializes in the treatment of dissociative disorders, ritual abuse trauma, and abused children and adults. She is an activist for survivors of ritual abuse and mind control.

"Louise" has survived severe abuse by means of dissociative identity disorder (DID). She speaks at training events for counsellors, therapists, and mental health professionals on various aspects of DID. She continues her journey towards healing, with all its challenges.

Warwick Middleton holds appointments as Adjunct Professor in the School of Public Health, La Trobe University, Melbourne, Australia, and Associate Professor in Psychiatry, University of Queensland. He has made substantial and ongoing contributions to the bereavement and trauma literatures and, with Jeremy Butler, authored the first published series in the Australian scientific literature detailing the abuse histories and clinical phenomenology of patients fulfilling diagnostic criteria for dissociative identity disorder. He chairs The Cannan Institute as well as its research and conference organizing committees. In 1996 he was a principle architect in establishing Australia's first dedicated unit treating dissociative disorders. He is also the director of the Trauma and Dissociation Unit, Belmont Hospital, Brisbane, and a member of the General Medical Assessment Tribunal, Queensland.

Phil Mollon is a psychoanalyst, psychotherapist, and clinical psychologist. He has written widely in the fields of trauma, shame, and narcissistic disturbance. He wrote the first British book exploring clinical aspects of dissociative identity disorder, *Multiple Selves, Multiple Voices* (1996). His other books have included *The Fragile Self* (1993), *Releasing the Self: The Healing Legacy of Heinz Kohut* (2001), and *Shame and Jealousy* (2002). In recent years he has become interested in highly effective adjunctive methods for treating trauma and anxiety, including EMDR, Thought Field Therapy, and the field known as "energy psychology". These latter explorations culminated in his latest book: *Psychoanalytic Energy Psychotherapy*

(2007). He works within the National Health Service in Hertford-shire and has a small private practice.

Bettina Overkamp is a psychologist and has worked in a trauma ambulance in a psychiatric clinic in Germany. She is a specialist in diagnostic issues and a member of the Executive Board of the European Society for Trauma and Dissociation (ESTD). She currently works in a hospital with acutely traumatized patients.

Carol Rutz is a healed ritual abuse/mind control survivor in the United States who works at endeavours that provide validation and healing for the survivor community. She is author of *A Nation Betrayed: The Chilling True Story of Secret Cold War Experiments Performed on Our Children and Other Innocent People* (2001).

Adah Sachs is a psychoanalytic psychotherapist and registered member of the Centre for Attachment-Based Psychoanalytic Psychotherapy. She works as a consultant psychotherapist at the Clinic for Dissociative Studies in London, a small specialist outpatient mental health service for people suffering from severe trauma and dissociation. She has worked for many years as a psychotherapist in psychiatric hospitals, with adults and adolescents. She is a visiting lecturer and a training supervisor at the Centre for Child Mental Health, the Institute for Arts in Psychotherapy and Education, and at the Centre for Attachment-Based Psychoanalytic Psychotherapy and maintains a small private practice.

John Silverstone has over thirty years of clinical experience. He gained a BSc in Physiology, then trained and worked in general nursing for twelve years. In 1981 he switched careers and trained as an osteopath. Since qualifying as an osteopath he has undertaken postgraduate training in osteopathy in the cranial field and more recently specialized in paediatric osteopathy. He taught on the undergraduate course at the British School of Osteopathy and currently contributes to postgraduate teaching on the MSc course for the Foundation for Paediatric Osteopathy.

Valerie Sinason is a poet, writer, child and adult psychotherapist, and adult psychoanalyst. She is currently Director of the Clinic for Dissociative Studies in London and Honorary Consultant

Psychotherapist to the University of Cape Town Child Guidance Clinic. She specializes in the areas of trauma, abuse, and disability and is President of the Institute for Psychotherapy and Disability. She has published 13 books and over 70 professional papers. Her books include *Mental Handicap and the Human Condition* (1992), *Treating Survivors of Satanist Abuse* (1994), *Memory in Dispute* (1998) and *Attachment, Trauma and Multiplicity: Working with Dissociative Identity Disorder* (2002). She has also published two volumes of poetry entitled *Inkstains & Stilettos* (1987) and *Night Shift* (1995).

FORENSIC ASPECTS OF
DISSOCIATIVE IDENTITY DISORDER

Introduction

Adah Sachs

L ily, 13, was the sweetest girl you can imagine. Big blue eyes, a lovely, soft smile, and a gentle voice. She was admitted following a massive overdose, as well as repeated episodes of head banging. At the time of her admission her forehead was so hugely swollen that she looked quite deformed. She appeared insightful regarding some school problems she had and was generally charming and warm, showing every sign of being a normal "troubled adolescent". That was rather at odds with the level of her self-harm and with our knowledge of severe abuse in her history. Lily, I might add, had maintained that "nothing bad had ever happened to her".

On her second session, Lily came wearing her hair in pigtails and holding her teddy, which made her look about 6 or 7 years old. Still at the door, she asked me sweetly if I'd look after her teddy for her. I asked if she felt that he needed help, too, and she said that we were all making a mistake: he was the one "in danger"; she was fine. At that, she sat on the floor, carefully placing the teddy on the patient's chair. After a moment of silence, she said she was very worried about him; he would die if he wasn't watched. I asked what did she fear may happen to him. To my shock, her sweet little face suddenly became white and contorted, and in a monstrous, croaking voice that sounded to me like it came straight from *The Exorcist*, she roared, "I–I–I–I will kill him!"

Now who is "I", and where does it live: in the teddy, which she had put on the patient's chair? In her harmed body? In the contorted faces of her abusers, who were suddenly visible on her own face? Or perhaps in that Lily she had told me about, the one whom "nothing bad had ever happened to"?

For Lily was actually many "Lily's", who were largely unaware of each other. Most of them were very distressed in different ways, but one of them was a bright and lovely girl, with some minor difficulties at school, who was completely baffled by her strangely swollen forehead and had no idea why she was in a hospital at all.

One night, with great consternation and rather shakily, a white-faced Lily told the ward nurses that she had murdered her sister. She was then sick and couldn't go back to sleep for a long time. The incident was recorded as "hallucination". But was it? She had never hallucinated before and did not again, to my knowledge, after that night. In a session she had with me some days later, she again alluded to that murder, adding her sister's name.

I was haunted by questions: Was it a phantasy? What does such phantasy mean? Did it express her secret wish to be rid of her sister? But her record showed that she was an only child. Did her mother know about these thoughts? Did the family therapist understand any more? Could it—could it possibly be true? Did I have a duty to report it? To whom? What would happen if it were true, and I treated it as a symbolic expression? Should I become Sherlock Holmes and try to investigate? What would happen to the therapeutic relationships? To the mother? To the girl? What would happen to me? Could I be prosecuted for withholding information about a serious crime? For disclosing confidential material? For wasting police time? For being stupid?

One of the most uncomfortable aspects of offering therapy to people with dissociative identity disorder (DID) is that, sooner or later, most of them begin to talk about horrendous crimes. Crimes that were committed against them, crimes that they have witnessed, or crimes that they have been made to commit or have deliberately committed themselves. The crimes that they describe are always shocking. They sound unlikely, mad, impossible. Almost always they are unproven, and there are so many bits missing in these stories that one can hardly think how they can ever be proven—or, for that matter, proven wrong.

Dissociative identity disorder (formerly known as multiple personality disorder), is a baffling, confusing and seemingly bizarre condition. Although DID is a formal *DSM–IV* diagnosis, it is very controversial, and many professionals hold the view that it is extremely rare, doesn't exist at all, or is factitious (pretended). I suspect that the most important reason for the reluctance to recognize DID is not its confusing appearance, which to many professionals is actually rather fascinating. I believe that the reluctance stems from the disturbing link between DID and the most extreme and sadistic forms of crime, especially when faced with the continued involvement that many survivors still have with a world that none of us wishes to believe in or to share (Coleman, chapter 1; Healey, chapter 2; Cross & "Louise", chapter 5; Silverstone, chapter 12; Cook, chapter 13).

There is, on the whole, a fair interest in the "mechanism" of dissociation, which is quite fascinating. Much less interest is usually found in the background to DID. Similarly, there is much more openness among therapists to techniques of "grounding" the traumatized person than there is to listening and bearing witness to a traumatic history. One may say that this is rather at odds with the normal therapeutic stance, which is that listening to and understanding the history of a patient are prerequisites to any helpful therapeutic process. I would like to highlight here the rather obvious fact that therapists, while aiming to help, are aided by—and hampered by—their own emotional and mental scope, not least by their capacity to hear evil.

Furthermore, therapists, on the whole, are interested in and are trained to delve deeply into the internal processes of the psyche. Our consulting room is deemed best used as a place for thinking, feeling, and reflecting, and what we normally hope for is an internal development or transformation. Being called upon to respond to serious, sometimes ongoing crimes is not usually our area of interest, training, skill, or competence. It forces our attention outwards rather than inwards. We become worried about our own responsibility for what was—or is—being done to, or by, our patient. We feel unsure whether what we hear is an internal, psychological process or whether it is in the external reality of the person (Sinason, chapter 7; Mollon, chapter 8). We get caught up in trying to figure out "what really happened" and in doubts about the truthfulness of the narratives that we hear. We feel guilty and anxious when we don't believe the person's story—and perhaps even more guilty and anxious when we do believe it, as this may mean that we should be doing something of which we aren't sure. Not to mention the anxieties about being simply wrong, misled, taken in. Of all the forensic stories that one may hear in the consulting room, the ones coming from people with DID are probably the most unbelievable, the most shockingly grotesque, and the least corroborated. It is not surprising that these accounts are met with a great deal of suspicion and often outright hostility; and the field of extreme trauma is marred by fierce political debates, aggressive legal battles (e.g. regarding false memories), and bitter professional disagreements, as if in resonance with the violent nature of the clinical material.

Whether one is a therapist, a police officer, a clergyman, a GP, or a lawyer, listening to accounts of people with DID is confusing, owing to the multiplicity of speakers and all the contradictions that arise from that. A person may relate an event, while another alter of that same person completely denies it, has a different version of what happened, or is shocked at the fact that you ask questions about a subject that she or he had never told you about and is a secret. One is forever left questioning: Does all this really happen (Coleman, chapter 1; Sinason, chapter 7)? What (and who, and if, and why) do I really believe? Does what I believe matter (Galton, chapter 9)? Is the person speaking responsible for the crimes that have, allegedly, been committed by other alters, and what are the implications of the answer (Farmer, Middleton, & Devereux, chapter 6)? What are the limits of confidentiality when an alter reports a crime, whether in the past, the present, or the future (Anderson, chapter 11; Cook, chapter 13)?

Perhaps even more than the minefield created by multiplicity and dissociation, DID is hard to engage with because it is very upsetting, frightening, and unnerving. The traumatic content of the stories is upsetting and frightening. The unproven claims about terrible crimes are unnerving. There is an overall sense of a big pitfall that one is constantly on the verge of, while grappling with difficult clinical, ethical, moral, and legal questions, not to mention the spiritual concern that many people feel about such a close brush with evil.

One can't help but wish for the problem to "go away", or be proven to be a mistake, a misunderstanding, hallucination, or lie. But it seems that rather than going away, our growing (if still rather limited) knowledge of extreme abuse and its sequels is pointing to the contrary. The results of the Extreme Abuse Surveys (Becker, Karriker, Overkamp, & Rutz, chapter 3) give a stark picture of the types of abuse that people with DID (and others) have reported.

Many authors discuss trauma and abuse as the cause of disso-ciative disorders: to name but a few, the *DSM–IV–TR* (APA, 2000), Ross (2000, 2004), Sinason (1994, 1998, 2002), Mollon (1996, 1998), van der Kolk, McFarlane, and Weisaeth (1996), and van der Hart, Nijenhuis, and Steele (2006). The most relevant point for this book is that none of these authors refers to trauma in general, such as may occur as a result of natural disasters, poverty, or hunger. They refer specifically to trauma that is deliberately and systematically inflicted by people on whom the victim is dependent, with the aim of creating intense suffering and intense fear and, subsequently, utter submission to the will of the perpetrators (Sachs, chapter 10; Sinason, chapter 14; Lacter, chapter 15). The perpetrators may be religious groups, paedophiles, political entities or simply a family ("Aahbee", chapter 4), as well as any combination of them. They all intend to achieve an invisible slavery that makes the victims unable to resist the wishes of the perpetrators, including participa-tion in further perpetration: indeed, another unnerving aspect of working with survivors of these types of abuse is the realization that, often, they are also the perpetrators of the awful crimes that they describe.

I'll return to my young patient, Lily.

Sadly, at the time that I attempted to treat her, I knew very lit-tle about this subject, and I was of very little help to her. I did not ask more about her sister, nor did I think that there might be other alters, inside Lily, who knew about things that she didn't know. Through several years of psychiatric admission, most of which were spent in intensive care, locked units, Lily has never been assessed for having a dissociative disorder of any kind. She had an array of other diagnoses and a poor treatment outcome. My own resistance to entertaining the possibility of a real, bizarre crime—a resistance that was totally supported by my entire professional environment—did not help her to explain. Her tormented world remained intact, unreachable, untouched by any understanding. And she was not the only one.

It is for the sake of reaching the many other Lilys out there that we need to think deeper.

* * *

The chapters in this book reflect the thoughts of a range of professionals who have worked with this group, as well as those of two people who have DID, about the forensic aspect of their experience.

Joan Coleman addresses the question that is always asked about organized abuse: "So why don't the police get them?" Her chapter is about the great difficulties of bringing cases of alleged satanist ritual abuse to court. She describes the low credibility of accounts regarding any satanist activity, as well as the further complication of having to rely on witnesses whose accounts are subject to change as their alters or personalities change.

Chris Healey, in an interview, takes us through his own vexing experience, questions, and quandaries in the process of investigating four allegations of ritual abuse that were made to the police by people with DID.

Thorsten Becker, Wanda Karriker, Bettina Overkamp, and Carol Rutz report the preliminary results of the largest survey to date of extreme abuse—the Extreme Abuse Surveys—reflecting a sample of over 2,000 survivors and professionals from 40 countries. From the responses to the survey's detailed questions, which cover many areas, the authors have extricated for this book the ones relating to forensic issues.

"Aahbee" writes about the development of her own DID in the traumatic environment of severe domestic abuse. She shares her insights into this process, which are based on her professional understanding as well as her personal therapeutic journey.

Sue Cross and "Louise", in a counsellor-and-survivor joint account, show the complex multidimensional maze of learning "what really happened" to "Louise", who spent three years in prison.

James Farmer, Warwick Middleton, and John Devereux write about the complex position of the law regarding *agency* and *responsibility* in cases of crimes that were committed by persons with DID. The principles on which responsibility is allocated, or is deemed "diminished", are discussed in a number of cases that have come to court in the United States, Australia, and New Zealand.

Valerie Sinason talks about the internal and external reality of murder in the life of a person with DID, in a rare case where a body was found and a conviction took place. In this surprising account, Sinason shows how the "internal" and the "external" are not mutually exclusive, and that the search for the truth is even more complex than may first meet the eye.

Phil Mollon's chapter is about the difficulties in offering psychoanalytic psychotherapy in cases where the horrendous internal reality is inextricably linked with the patient's external reality.

Graeme Galton explores the clinical implications of the psychotherapist maintaining a strictly neutral stance on the question of believing—or not—the DID patient's memories of extreme abuse and the effect that this stance is likely to have on the patient. He considers the meaning of believing not just the psychic reality of the patient's account, but also the historical truth of what the patient is saying.

Adah Sachs offers a theoretical link between extreme abuse and DID, using a new attachment theory classification, *infanticidal attachment*, and considers the idea that the very presence of DID may serve as forensic evidence.

Alison Anderson shares her sense of professional isolation and clinical concerns regarding a patient with DID whom she treats in general practice.

John Silverstone considers trauma evidence in the body, through the eye of an osteopath. He describes his findings when examining people with DID and their distinctive kind of presentation, differentiating old, new, and repeated injuries, as well as "scars" that are left in the body tissues as a result of intense emotional trauma.

Sue Cook grapples with some of the ethical and practical difficulties of counselling a person who is repeatedly assaulted—and perhaps who is assaulting—while in therapy.

Valerie Sinason, in her second chapter, looks at the phenomenon of mind control as one of the ways in which DID is deliberately produced. Sinason discusses mind control in its wider social context, from the normal to the sinister.

Ellen Lacter offers a description of twelve different types of mind control, from the simplest and conscious to the most complex and unconscious. She then discusses methods for "undoing" the control over the person's mind in an attempt to restore the capacity for thinking freely.

* * *

Dissociative identity disorder is considered to be very difficult to treat. In looking at the forensic side of this disorder, I hope to highlight what, to my mind, makes it so difficult: the terror, the secrets, and the defensive (or protective) chasm between the traumatized person and all those who have not been tortured. I believe that reaching across this chasm is the true work of integration.

This is the aim of this book.

CHAPTER ONE

Satanist ritual abuse and the problem of credibility

Joan Coleman

"All that is necessary for the triumph of evil is that good men do nothing."

Edmund Burke, *Reflections on the Revolution in France*, 1790

D
o some satanists really commit crimes and abuse children? Many people believe not. My own hard-earned professional experience tells me otherwise.

This chapter is an account of my own journey: a journey from relative ignorance prior to 1980, through growing awareness of the extent of child sexual abuse, through my bizarre, frightening introduction to satanist ritual abuse, to my eventual belief that satanist crime does, indeed, occur. And I would like to think that mine is a reflective, rather than reflexive, belief (van der Hart & Nijenhuis, 1999)—that is, belief that stems from reflecting on the evidence, rather than blind acceptance of what initially seems highly improbable.

Ritual abuse evoked considerable interest in Britain between 1987 and 1994. The subject was taken up by many professionals, mainly psychologists, counsellors, and social workers; numerous children thought to be at risk were taken into care. In 1989, some of us who had encountered it formed an organization called RAINS (Ritual Abuse Information Network & Support), with the aim of sharing information and supporting each other.

Ritual abuse can be found in a wide range of social and religious backgrounds. In this chapter, I focus on abuse within satanist groups, as that is the type that I myself and most RAINS members have largely encountered.

In 1990, the National Society for the Prevention of Cruelty to Children (NSPCC) issued a press release regarding the large number of such cases they were working with. There were numerous press articles and several television programmes. In 1991, Health Secretary Virginia Bottomley appointed an anthropologist, Professor Jean La Fontaine, to research the subjects of organized and ritual abuse. La Fontaine had already written an acclaimed book on child sexual abuse.

In the summary of her report, La Fontaine concluded that there was no evidence of satanist abuse and that the alleged disclosures of the children were largely suggested by adults. In those cases in which the police had found "satanic" paraphernalia, she maintained that these were simply used by paedophiles to intimidate the children (Great Britain, Dept. of Health, 1994).

Largely as a result of this report, both the media and professionals became cautious about the subject of ritual abuse, and many shied away from it. Social workers were instructed not to mention the words "ritual" or "satanic" in any reports regarding child abuse.

Meanwhile, an increasing number of adults were seeking help with what they were convinced were genuine memories of severe and sadistic abuse that they had undergone as children. The recognition of the reality of child sexual abuse and its resulting psychological effects enabled adult survivors of satanist ritual abuse to feel some hope that they would be believed. However, this was not always the case because when ceremonies and sacrifices were mentioned, these were dismissed by some psychiatrists as delusions and many survivors were given inappropriate treatment with antipsychotic drugs. The False Memory Syndrome Foundation (set up in 1992) and the British False Memory Society (set up in 1993) also contributed to the general attitude of scepticism among professionals, and the whole subject of ritual crime became "suspect".

Incidentally, the reader may notice that I have been using the term "satanist" rather than the more commonly used "satanic". In my view, it is important to make this distinction because, although the alleged abuse may be done in the name of Satan, whom the abusers profess to worship, it is nonetheless people, not Satan, who are the abusers.

From ignorance, through uncertainty, to reflective belief

When I was working towards membership of the Royal College of Psychiatrists in the early 1970s, only a few days of the course were dedicated to the subject of sexual disorders, which included perversions and fetishisms, incest, and paedophilia. The latter was considered rare and usually referred to strange men preying on children singly, rather than in groups. When the existence of the Paedophile Information Exchange network was exposed less than a decade later, it was an eye-opener for many that a large number of professional people appeared to be abusing on an organized scale. Furthermore, most of us were still unaware of the extent of child sexual abuse by family members.

Margaret

In the autumn of 1986 my comfortable world was shattered and has never been the same since. I had by then been working in a psychiatric hospital for nearly 17 years. One of my wards was for patients with both physical and psychiatric disorders. One such patient, a woman in her early forties, whom I will call Margaret, had been admitted frequently to the ward during the previous four years. I was aware that her physical illnesses—asthma, peptic ulceration, and severe migraines—were connected with her mental disturbances, but I was unable to identify the cause of these. She had plenty of visitors, and she denied any family problems.

She was given to self-harm—mainly overdosing with prescribed drugs—especially during weekend leave. On one occasion that summer, she overdosed within hours of discharge and returned to hospital the following day via the Accident & Emergency Department. Her physical condition rapidly deteriorated, and by the autumn she was vomiting blood.

Soon after this, in response to an almost casual question about her clear dislike of a family friend, she began talking, and the floodgates on her disclosures opened. As well as talking to me, she also talked to Eileen, a nurse whom she trusted, and we started to work with her together.

Initially she spoke of what appeared to be a large paedophile network that was currently active. She described sadistic sexual abuse of children by men; some of these men were members of her family and their acquaintances, some were politicians, some were well-known entertainers.

From the time of her first disclosures, there was a remarkable improvement in her physical symptoms. The vomiting ceased, and she had no further asthma or migraine attacks. She stopped overdosing and seemed ready to continue talking. At times she would confuse and exasperate us by saying that she had made it up, but within hours she would withdraw this. Eileen and I knew little about paedophile networks, but we agreed that we would withhold judgement and just record everything that we were told.

We decided that, whether or not she was telling the truth, we should involve the police, which was done at a fairly early stage. However, when the names of alleged abusers were not found on criminal record files, police interest waned. We were told that if we could provide some evidence, they would then investigate.

In the early summer of 1987, Margaret, who was still an inpatient, learned that she had a terminal illness. She reacted to this by insisting on her discharge, saying she wanted to die at home. When I expressed doubt about the wisdom of this, she retracted all her disclosures, maintaining that she had always been given to fantasy and had made the whole thing up. This left us with mixed feelings: relief that these horrors were possibly not real, anger at having been "taken for a ride", and yet still feeling considerable doubt about what really was the truth. Was there pressure on her to retract, or did she just want to spend her last few years in peace?

Within a few weeks of discharge she was back, having been found in a drugged state staggering among traffic. She was now detained under Section 3 of the Mental Health Act, which, unless she was discharged by a tribunal, would detain her in hospital for six months. Possibly this enabled her to feel safe enough to extend her previous disclosures. At all events, she began to give detailed descriptions of runaway children being met at the big London stations and offered accommodation in what they were told was a hostel. There they were forced to take drugs to which they quickly became addicted. Soon they were being abused and hired out for sex. She then described another house to which some of these children, mainly boys, were taken. She commented on how they initially appeared normal but were taken out of the room only to be brought back limp and drooping. Later, we learned that some children are given muscle relaxants prior to abuse, but at that time we had no knowledge of such things. What puzzled us more was why Margaret was taken to witness these activities. She explained that whenever she had protested about what went on, she was forced to watch and was photographed to maintain her silence.

Photographs were also taken of the abuse, she said. After being raped or buggered by a number of men, some of the children were returned to the "hostel". Others were killed. This, she told us, was always done with a knife. The body was then dismembered and the parts enclosed in plastic bags, which were taken to what she described as a factory, where they were disposed of in vast kilns. The killings were recorded on videos, which were sold for huge sums as "snuff movies". She described the same pattern each time and commented that "it seemed like some sort of ritual". Even then we did not grasp what she was trying to tell us. Not until she spoke of abusers wearing robes and masks and young Vietnamese children being tied to altars and inverted crosses did we begin to understand and research what was written about satanism and satanist ritual abuse. Later, she admitted that her family had been satanists for generations. Thereafter, there were no further retractions, and we felt, for the first time, that her accounts were adding up. But because we now believed her, it was all the more terrifying for us.

Her mental health improved markedly after these disclosures, and, when her detention under the Mental Health Act was lifted, she was discharged and needed no further admissions. We continued to see her regularly as an outpatient.

Following the disclosures that children were being killed, we involved the police a second time. We supplied them with names and addresses of more alleged perpetrators and with more details regarding the children. By the time they called us back to tell us the result of their investigation, Margaret had divulged a great deal more about cult activities, including descriptions of ceremonies, locations, and hierarchy. She made a clear distinction between the killings of the children in London and the ceremonial sacrifices. The former, she said, were sadistic and commercial; the latter, however, were part of a religious ceremony in which both men and women participated. These sacrifices were always performed by the High Priest on certain festival dates. Their purpose was to enhance the power of the cult.

We were prepared to give all our information to the police and had already provided the address of the "factory". They told us they had found some bricked-up areas there and had even contacted the bricklayers, who told them these had formerly held windows, not kilns. The police, meanwhile, had appointed an independent psychiatrist to interview Margaret. The psychiatrist's conclusions were that I had invented the whole story and persuaded her that satanism was the background to all her problems, whereas he attributed them to the repressive attitude of a strict aunt who had lived with her during her childhood. The Assistant Chief Constable accepted his opinion but did not report me to the General Medical Council, as the psychiatrist had requested. The Detective Chief Superintendent who had conducted the investigation gave me his personal phone number, saying he wished to be kept informed. Unfortunately, he retired from the police force not long after.

From September 1988 onwards, Eileen and I continued listening to and recording Margaret's disclosures without further police involvement. She described the methods of mind control used by cults; how children were drugged and hypnotized to believe in the magical power of Satan. Despite her awareness of the deception of children, she still half-believed in this magic. She claimed to have actually seen Satan and demons at some ceremonies. Not until she was taken to a ceremony a year or so later, did she become less credulous. She decided to watch events carefully instead of staring at the candles, as instructed. She observed both "Satan" and "demons" appearing from behind a screen. After that, she gradually ceased to believe that there was any supernatural aspect to cult activity. She thus became much less fearful and considerably stronger. On ceremony dates she would barricade her room, refusing to attend. Occasionally, she was punished, but the perpetrators knew of the police involvement, which ensured her safety.

Eventually she was left alone by the cult. She got herself a job and became independent. Sadly, by the time she died a few years later, she had, for the first time, developed a zest for life. She just described it as "Sod's Law".

Margaret was one of the most courageous women whom I have met. Eileen and I saw her just hours before she died. She repeated that everything she had told us about the cult was true and that she wanted everyone to know.

Theresa

By the late 1980s, we had become aware of other cases alleging satanist ritual abuse. We made efforts to contact the professionals involved and listen to their accounts. Many of these cases had already been heard in the criminal or family courts, so there was no question of contaminating evidence. We thus became acquainted with a small network of people who had encountered satanist ritual abuse. In early 1989, I was asked by one of these professionals if I would work with a 15-year-old girl who was claiming satanist abuse by members of her extended family from whom she had escaped 18 months earlier.

This girl described cult activities in a much more direct manner than Margaret, but the procedures, including the methods of abusing children, were almost identical. She provided much detail about a large, castle-like house, to which she and other children were taken regularly. They were drugged before the journey, so she had no idea of its whereabouts. She believed it to be owned by a doctor, because part of the basement was used for experimental operations. Another part, she claimed, contained small cult children who were kept in cages, brought out only for abuse, operations, and ultimately, sacrifice. She also talked of a large tub of acid, which was used for disposal of the bodies. She seemed determined to tell everything she knew.

In this case, the police were already involved and had charged five men with rape of a minor and one woman with aiding and abetting and with procuring an abortion. Although Theresa had spoken of them to the police, there was no evidence available to prove the ritual activities, so these were omitted from the charges. Shortly before the trial, the police visited her school to obtain records of her attendance. The school counsellor then gave them some notes and drawings that Theresa had produced some months earlier, when she was upset by memories of what she had witnessed. These included a graphic description of the ritual sacrifice of a tramp.

A few days before the trial was due to start, there was great consternation within the Crown Prosecution Service, because they had seen this material. The prosecution lawyers had no choice but to inform the defence lawyers. After a morning of deliberation, the case was adjourned. I was then asked to write a full report including all that she had disclosed regarding the cult activities and sacrifices. As a result, the prosecution lawyers maintained that there was no chance of any jury believing it, so, at the next court appearance, they offered no evidence and the defendants walked free.

This case well illustrates the difficulty with credibility. Even now, 17 years later, prosecution lawyers are reluctant to include details of a ritual aspect in cases involving sexual abuse of, or cruelty towards, children. That is because it is not illegal in the United Kingdom to practice satanism, nor to wear gowns or masks. Therefore, such material coming up in court is not only considered irrelevant, it seriously undermines the credibility of any other account of the witness.

This situation might well change if tangible evidence were more forthcoming, but until there is generalized acceptance of the reality of satanist ritual abuse, the evidence will not be sought. It is a vicious circle.

After the collapse of the court case, I continued working with

Theresa. I am happy to say that she became increasingly strong. The abusers eventually stopped all attempts at harassment, and she was able to lead a normal life. She is now a healthy young woman with a husband and family. We have remained close friends.

* * *

Difficult as it was to cross the barrier of their seemingly incredible stories, and my own doubt, when working with my first two survivors of satanist ritual abuse, it could have been even harder. I was fortunate, for example, that neither one of them had disclosed recovered memories: it was clear that they had never forgotten. I know that I did not suggest or induce these memories. In Margaret's case, my knowledge was so scant that I would not have known what to suggest. In Theresa's case, she had already disclosed much of the material to others before I knew her.

Neither of these two survivors showed evidence of dissociative identity disorder, then known as multiple personality disorder. Both described and occasionally displayed episodes of dissociation, but these subsided soon after they were free from cult activity. I had heard that multiple personality disorder was common in cult victims who were abused from birth, but I found this concept hard to accept. Not until I started working with my third satanist abuse survivor was I confronted with this baffling condition; after that, there was no mistaking it.

Monica

In late 1990 I had a call from a counselling community psychiatric nurse asking for advice about a 37-year-old woman named Monica who had been referred to her by a health visitor a few months earlier because she was bulimic. Monica was now disclosing ritual abuse since babyhood. Mandy, the community psychiatric nurse, felt in need of some help, so I started to see Monica with her on alternate sessions. Occasionally, when Mandy was away, I saw her alone.

At first, she was terrified of talking about the cult, but after a few weeks she started to give detailed accounts of her memories.

She talked more about her childhood than had Margaret, who had concentrated on what was happening to children currently. Many of Monica's memories were re-lived and described in child-like voices with similar facial expressions and mannerisms. These child-like parts of her maintained that they had different names and ages, and sometimes, when she wrote, it was in the script of a 5-year-old. At other times, she seemed unlike her usual self and was quite hostile towards Mandy and myself. It gradually emerged that some of her personalities were still fiercely loyal to the cult. While Monica herself believed she had not been involved with cult activities since she was 15 years old, some of her personalities had never stopped being linked to it and had no intention of leaving. These personalities were still regularly attending cult meetings, without her having any knowledge of it.

This was my initiation to DID, and although Monica, too, sadly died some years later, I shall always be grateful to her. She taught both Mandy and myself an enormous amount—not only regarding cult practices, but how to work with alters who were still loyal to the cult.

Both Margaret and Theresa had spoken of childhood "marriages to Satan"—although Theresa referred to him as Lucifer. These marriages involved taking vows of loyalty to Satan and the cult. There were threats of severe punishment if these were broken. They were told that the cult would know by magical means if they were talking. Monica also spoke of these vows, and many of her alters still believed in the magic. She emphasized, too, as had the others, that children are forced to become perpetrators, even at the age of 4 years. This instils guilt into them, which enhances control by the cult. She also explained how children were tortured, as a means of inducing alters that would be loyal to the cult. At the height of the torture, they would be given a new name and told that if ever this name was called, they were to come up and obey instructions. Incredible as this sounds, it is very similar to some of the mind-control programming performed during the Cold War. The de-programming of these alters took considerable time and involved her re-living the painful memory of when they were induced, in order for her to understand the extent of her deception by the cult.

As the years went by, the amnesic barriers that made her alters unaware of each others' existence and actions gradually broke down. She became increasingly aware of her own degree of involvement with the cult, as well as that of others. She provided names of members and locations of cult meetings. Although I had told her nothing about other survivors, some of these corresponded not only with those given by Margaret, but also with details concerning cases in the late 1980s. She spoke of the High Priest by his cult name, but also told us his real name. I had neither heard of him nor seen photographs, although he carried out an important national function. One day there was an article in a newspaper in which this man was named and his professional work indicated. The accompanying photograph showed a nondescript elderly man sitting among several others at a bus stop. I copied the picture, removing all the script, and showed it to Monica, asking if any of these people were familiar. She immediately pointed to the man, saying "That's _____" (mentioning his cult name). This provided even more credibility to her account.

One of her alters was a 10-year-old, who gloried in the name of Scumbag. She had first appeared when Monica was 10 and was hired out by her mother to "service" men in the backroom of a pub. The money earned was collected up for her mother, thence handed to the cult. Scumbag was not induced but appeared naturally, in order to protect Monica from these rough men. Not surprisingly, she was a great beer drinker, whereas Monica herself drank no alcohol. She was very forthright in her accounts and was able to provide much information about people, locations, and crimes committed. She became my particular friend, and I believe she was entirely truthful.

Monica was another courageous woman. She spoke out on a radio programme in 1996, and for this she was punished. This almost certainly led to her death a short time later.

* * *

Coincidental with Monica, and after her death, I worked with a number of others who described crimes and practices very similar to those already mentioned. I hold the phone line for RAINS and therefore receive calls from many therapists seeking help and advice. Their clients talk of the same activities. Although RAINS is an organization for professionals, we also get requests for help from many survivors of satanist ritual abuse. I never divulge my knowledge of cults, yet their accounts are usually remarkably similar.

Most survivors of alleged generational satanism are very clear that it is not simply a matter of attending satanist ceremonies, but a way of life. Much of the abuse is carried out at home, often by their mothers; it involves every aspect of life, including the food given to the children, which may contain raw animal flesh or insects. Spiders play a large part with most of these children, who are taught that they are Satan's agents and will report any misdemeanours, and also that if they are eaten, as the children are often forced to do, they will multiply within and watch them from inside.

Elaine

Mooch is a 16-year-old alter who wants me to write about her case. Mooch is not the name of my current client, a woman in her fifties whom I will call Elaine. Mooch is determined to expose what is happening, and she reckons that, "They won't learn anything they don't already know." She was induced by the cult through torture when my client was a child of 12. She was given the name Miranda. Initially, she grew older with Elaine, but at 16 she decided to be independent of the group and to change her name to Mooch. This was only partially successful because she had previously been persuaded through hypnosis that she was deeply in love with her "keeper" in the cult and that her love was reciprocated, despite him treating her with extreme brutality. Thus he maintained control over her for many years. Happily, she is no longer under his spell.

Mooch is the one who is now normally present and carries out many day-to-day activities. She is a pretty tough character who protects the little ones and will stand no nonsense. She has no direct memories of Elaine's early life, but those alters who do remember have told her much of what took place, so she is knowlededgeable about their life as a whole.

Another part of Elaine, who remembers a great deal as well as knowing what happens currently, is a 5-year-old girl called Reggie. Her speech, writing, and spelling are those of her age, but her capability is vast. She knows when to keep secrets and hide things that might upset or trigger the other alters. She passes all these on to me later. A police officer who interviewed her a few years back asked her whether she knew the difference between truth and lies. She looked at him very solemnly and said, "I never tell fibs." I believe that. She looks after the other child alters and spends much time cooking, embroidering, and gardening. They all agree they could not do without her.

All the crimes spoken of by previous clients and telephone contacts have also been described by Mooch, Reggie, and other alters. These include severe and sadistic sexual abuse; rape of children and adults; physical torture; impregnation and abortion of teenage girls; child and adult abduction and imprisonment; deception, brainwashing, and mind control; cruelty to animals; bestiality; and the murder of babies, children, and adults—the latter not always as "sacrifice to Satan", but often for punishment, in which case it is preceded by extreme torture. Mooch has also emphasized the extent of extortion that is carried out, to help fund the cult. Even victims on benefits are expected to "pay their dues" and are punished if they refuse. Money is obtained, too, from large-scale drug trafficking, together with enforced prostitution of both children and adults and the sale of child and adult pornography. Margaret is not alone in mentioning "snuff videos". Both Monica and Mooch have witnessed their production. If any prominent member of society—not necessarily in the cult—makes use of those children used for prostitution, then they are subsequently blackmailed.

When I first met Elaine in the late 1990s, she still had many alters who were loyal to the cult and were attending ceremonies and other cult activities. At that time, she was amnesic of these events. Frequently on these occasions she was injured; there would be heavy bruising and cuts on the front and back of her body. There were also satanist symbols branded there. All these were photographed and given to the police, who were involved before I knew her and were taking it seriously. Eventually, they sent the photographs to a forensic pathologist. Several physicians and surgeons had maintained that these injuries could not have been self-inflicted, but the pathologist, nonetheless, concluded that they were. That ended the police interest for the time being. Later, after the death of her father, who had lived with her and was not an abuser, she became even more vulnerable, as cult members now had access to her house. More injuries were inflicted and photographed. Numerous letters and occult artefacts were deposited in her house and garden, all of which were in turn handed to the police. No investigation took place. Different officers are now in charge of the investigation, and there appears to be some renewal of interest in this case.

Over the last three years she has made tremendous progress and shown great courage. We have worked with many cult-loyal alters, who have, one by one, come over to help her, having recognized their deception during their induction. Except on rare occasions, cult members are no longer able to gain access to her house or take her to ceremonies, and even their attempts at extortion usually fail. They continue trying to trigger her into a response, but so far without success.

* * *

I hope that these brief accounts regarding Margaret, Theresa, Monica, and Elaine give a flavour of the scope of the criminal activity alleged within some satanist cults. They may also help to illustrate the enormous difficulties regarding gathering evidence and thus establishing credibility.

People do not want to believe that such horrors take place in their own backyard. It is accepted that weird activities occur in certain African states, even that Africans in Britain may carry out strange practices. But ordinary British men and women? Not possible!

Most people believe that children and adults are sometimes raped, also that some people are sexually aroused by torture and pornography, and that others practice extortion and blackmail. It is also acknowledged that some people worship Satan. Why is it unbelievable that all these might sometimes be combined? Until the professionals concerned accept that satanist ritual abuse—or any kind of ritual abuse—is a reality, it will continue unabated, as it has for centuries past.

CHAPTER TWO

Unsolved:
investigating allegations of ritual abuse

An interview with Chris Healey

C*an you tell us about your first experience as a police officer investigating an allegation of ritual abuse?*

It was about 17 years ago. The carer of a young woman wrote to the police with a complaint saying that a crime the young woman had reported had not been investigated. My senior officer, who was the Head of the Criminal Investigation Department (CID), asked me to follow it up.

I went to meet the young woman, who was 24 years old, and interviewed her and her carer. I had two meetings with the young woman and took a lengthy statement from her. She told me that when she was 16 she came to the area and was homeless. She was picked up by two men who gained her confidence, gave her a room, and later sexually assaulted her, then introduced her to ritual abuse. She was able to name some of the people involved in the abuse. I checked the names she gave me, and these people did exist. One of them was a doctor and another was a senior police-man. I was rather doubtful that the latter would be involved in such practices, but this was what she told me.

During the interviews it became clear to me that the young woman was alcoholic, which is not necessarily a problem for an investigation provided that you're open about it in court, but it does nothing to help the credibility of a witness. In addition, the carer told me that the young woman had dissociative identity disorder and had several personalities, but I did not see any of them during my interviews with her.

As part of my investigation, during which eventually she stated that she had reported the sexual assaults to the local police, I checked the report of the crimes. It turned out that her report had, in fact, been investigated and two arrests had been made. The case had gone to the Crown Prosecution Service, but they had decided that there was insufficient evidence to proceed further. I also found that she had not told the original investigating officer about the ritual aspect of the crimes—she had only mentioned the sexual assault.

I was given quite a lot of freedom by my boss with my enquiries, so I set about investigating the woman's allegations further. Unfortunately, in the end I could not find sufficient new evidence, and that was what I eventually had to report. I did look at locations where rituals allegedly had taken place, but there were no traces, although they were areas where, according to local legend, rituals were performed.

The case was subsequently reopened, but those enquiries also got no further. Some time after my involvement with this case, a man confessed to a social worker that he had committed a murder. The social worker reported the claim to the police, and it was investigated. The man that he confessed to having murdered was one of the people who had been named by the young woman as being an abuser of young people and of being involved in rituals. Although no body was found, there was circumstantial evidence that he had been killed. There was forensic physical evidence that the man reported murdered had been at the top of a cliff, because traces of his DNA were found there. The man who confessed to the murder went to prison for the crime, but no evidence emerged relating to other aspects of the young woman's allegations.

I'm fairly convinced that what the young woman had reported about the sexual abuse was true, and the initial investigating officer had thought the same. However, I'm not so sure about the ritual abuse. Another officer later investigated the claims again, but got no further, and the case remains unresolved.

Not enough evidence—is this a common problem with ritual abuse allegations?

Yes. In most cases that I am aware of, it has not even been possible to identify the perpetrators, much less find evidence against them. In this case, the young woman had identified them, which is unusual. It's unfortunate that we could not find any other evidence to corroborate her claims.

What do you think about this kind of allegation?

I'm fairly open-minded. Anything is possible, but we need to find evidence in order to prove it. I found the allegation intriguing, and I have been involved in similar cases since.

Can you tell us about the next case of this type that you were involved with?

A woman who was under the care of a Community Psychiatric Nurse (CPN) reported to the nurse that she was being ritually abused and that the abuse was ongoing. I interviewed the woman who was making the allegation, with the CPN present. She gave me a lot of background information and names, but she could not identify the perpetrators in a way that made it possible for me to trace them.

One of the things she told me was that many years earlier she had been at a ceremony in some woodland during which a baby had been killed. She was able to take me to the place and identify the spot where the baby had been buried some 15 or 20 years previously. I asked my boss for permission to dig up the area, and he let me do it. We conducted a thorough search, but nothing was found, no baby's body. I spoke to the woman again, and she could not explain why we had not found anything. However, she later told the CPN that she had only been testing me to see if I believed her story. I had made a big investment in police time and money, and I was not pleased to be tested in this manner.

I stayed in contact with the nurse, and the woman passed on items through her that were allegedly connected with the rituals. Like the woman in the first case, this woman had DID. Among the items passed to me was a brooch that she said was a trigger mechanism for bringing out particular personalities. She also talked about something that she called the "Book of Shadows". She said it was her uncle who had introduced her to the group.

On one occasion, she told me that she was going to be taken to a ceremony some distance from her home and hurt. She was able to tell where she would be taken and when. I told her that we would keep her under surveillance and keep her safe, and I did alert police colleagues in the area where she said the ceremony would be held. On the weekend when the ceremony was allegedly going to happen, she decided not to go. I have to admit that I was not surprised. I did not think she was being entirely truthful. I was not told by my colleagues about any unusual activity in the area either.

I wonder what your colleagues think of all this, and of you?

Police officers come across many bizarre things in the course of their careers. However, you need to have an element of belief to get support for an investigation, because the police force is tied down by budgets and priorities. When we were digging up the woods, they asked me, "Do you believe her?" My answer was, "We won't know whether she is telling the truth until we look." Digging up a patch of ground is relatively low-risk, by which I mean it is not too manpower-intensive. On the other hand, surveillance is high-risk, because it's very expensive and you are taking resources from other investigations. I was glad that in this case I had not requested a surveillance operation.

You mentioned that this woman also had DID, like the first one. How many people with DID do you think you've met?

I think I've met five people with DID, all in connection with investigations of ritual abuse. Four of them were women, and one was a man. I've only actually seen them switch personalities in one case. I could see her change—it was absolutely extraordinary.

How did you learn about DID?

While I was conducting the first investigation I mentioned, I was advised to contact a particular psychiatrist who was an expert on DID. I thought it would be helpful for me to have some background from an independent point of view, someone who was not involved with the case and not involved with the young woman who made the allegations. This psychiatrist explained what DID was and told me about cases she was involved with. She taught me a lot. We have remained in contact, and our paths have crossed several times since then. It was through her that I came to investigate my third case, which also involved a woman with DID.

A woman told the psychiatrist that she was being taken out regularly and hurt, and that people were leaving dead animals on her doorstep. I arranged for fixed cameras to be put in place that would show anyone coming or going from her house. I did not tell her or the psychiatrist that I was doing this. Two weeks later the woman reported that she had been taken out and hurt again. But when we looked at the tapes, we could see no evidence for anything she'd described. I discussed it with the psychiatrist, who was quite taken aback and asked the woman about it. The woman said that she had left the house by another route, through a window, and that was why the camera had missed it.

Nonetheless, I'm convinced that this woman was telling me the truth, at least as she believed it, but I do not believe she went out through the window as she claimed. There is no doubt in my mind that she was sexually abused as a child. And, clearly, she was still receiving injuries. Her psychiatrist had photographed the injuries, and I sent the photographs to be examined by an independent forensic pathologist. To my surprise, I must say, he concluded that they could have been self-inflicted, even though some of them were on her back. I would not have thought it was possible, but I had to accept his expert opinion. I'm sceptical about what the woman claimed was happening in the present. I think that there was definitely something traumatic that had happened to her in the past which had caused her to develop DID. She was stuck with the thoughts of the trauma and believed that harmful things were still happening to her in the present. Her current injuries might be self-inflicted, as the forensic pathologist said. Of course, I can't be sure about this, but to me this seems the most likely explanation.

Have you ever come across a case of ritual abuse allegation that was proven?

No, I've never come across a case of ritual abuse that was proven. People have been named, but it's not been possible to identify them. Usually the name cannot be traced, the address does not exist, or the phone number is wrong. I've been looking for 15 years, and I've tried very hard to find proof. I've dug up fields, set up cameras, and looked down wells where bones were supposed to have been thrown, and I've found nothing that can be independently linked to the allegations.

So are you saying that ritual abuse allegations always end in a dead end?

Yes, in my experience, these allegations have always ended in a dead end.

When ritual abuse allegations are made, are the stories that people bring quite similar?

Yes, they are. And that's one of the most intriguing things about these bizarre allegations. There are common features:

> The person making the claims is called back to be abused by the main perpetrator.
> There is a ritual element in the stories—for example, the abuse is done at certain times of the year.
> Most of the claims involve the death of a child or a baby.
> Unregistered births are mentioned, with the explanation that this is how babies can be used and killed in rituals.
> There is drinking of blood.
> A "Book of Shadows" is mentioned.
> The person making the claims is phobic of certain things—for example, spiders.
> A doctor and a police officer are often claimed to be involved.

And there are other elements, too, that match down to quite small details. The repetition is very intriguing. These people are from all over the country, and unlikely to know each other—so how

come their stories are so similar? The obvious explanation is that
something similar did actually happen to them.

*And yet there has never been any proof. How do you explain that to
yourself?*

I'm pretty sure that these people have undergone a traumatic
experience at some time in their lives. They have been so traumatized by it that they live on with it. They've had some horrific
experience within the family. I think it has to have been within the
family, because if it was a stranger it would have been more likely
to have been reported at the time it happened. Maybe they bottle
it up and it develops into DID.

Sometimes I think that what was done to them was not necessarily ritualistic, but then I can't explain why their stories are all
so remarkably similar.

*So you think it is likely that something does, or at least did happen. Why,
then, is it so impossible to find any evidence?*

Maybe it's not happening. After the conviction of Rose and Fred
West, I was not surprised to hear claims that people had been
abused by them. That is quite common: people who are notorious
in public life tend to get allegations against them. But nothing was
heard about the Wests before they were caught.

If a large number of people are all keeping the secret, that's
a massive conspiracy, which is really hard to believe. Is it really
possible for a secret to be so perfectly well-kept? Why is there not
a twinge of conscience from one of these people in one of these
groups that leads to them revealing the secret?

*Could it be that their decision to talk to the police at all is that "twinge
of conscience"?*

Yes, maybe it is, but then they get cold feet and don't follow it
through with anything that can definitively prove an offence.

*Would you say that people with DID make poor informers and wit-
nesses?*

They are difficult witnesses to deal with, and they are unreliable
in court. If one personality is saying yes and another personality

is saying no, how do you take it to court? The Crown Prosecution Service would be reluctant to go to court if the witness was likely to change their evidence, because if they did that, the case would fall.

If traumatized people, especially with DID, are generally not good at providing evidence, can there ever be a way to prove such a case?

Advances in forensic science will perhaps mean that police can gather corroborating physical evidence, so that the prosecution would not have to rely solely on an unreliable witness. There have been huge advances in this area just in the last few years. Police are solving quite a number of old murders and rapes because of new scientific techniques. But that can only happen if the physical evidence was properly gathered in the first place. For example, when the baby was not found, it could have been because babies' bones are very soft and have disintegrated; but through more advanced methods it may still be possible to show that there had been remains there.

Of course, gathering physical evidence relies on there being a police officer who considers that such allegations may be true, and who is prepared to ask his boss to invest time and money on it. Is that asking a lot of a police officer?

I was lucky to work in a fairly unrestrained and informal way. That would be much more difficult to do now, in the present performance regime, where time is concentrated on the key performance indicators. Everything the police does now has to be clearly directed towards meeting key performance indicators. Everything has to be written down. All police activity has to be supported by a senior officer. Every interview of a serious offence is analysed, and a decision is made whether or not to investigate it further. If it sounds too bizarre, it might not be pursued. These days a Head of CID would probably say that it would be mad to pursue such an unlikely allegation.

On the other hand, the new stricter procedures may make it more likely to get these crimes investigated, because there is no easy way for police to dismiss a report of a crime. An investigating officer would have to take it to a senior officer; there would be a record of what investigation had taken place so far; there would have to be a written rationale behind every case where the decision was not to investigate. It is less likely, today, for a crime report to be lost in the system.

What is your advice to a psychotherapist, doctor, or social worker whose patient tells him or her about being ritually abused?

Get as much of the story as possible in a coherent form, if possible in writing. If possible, bring physical evidence, such as photographs or potential forensic evidence, to support the allegations. Cases are not likely to make it to court unless there is corroborating evidence, especially with unreliable witnesses.

Go to the police with your patient and present the story and the evidence to the police. You have to talk to a detective of reasonable rank, a sergeant, at least. Within 72 hours of someone reporting a crime, the police have to formally record it. There is a procedure, and they have to see that the report is properly investigated. They are then obliged to do something with it: either by investigating it further, or deciding no crime has been committed, or deciding to take no further action. I suggest that after reporting the crime, it is best to leave it a short time, then contact the police and enquire how the investigation is proceeding; in probability, though, they will contact you fairly soon with an update on decisions made.

Most police officers—and I think maybe most people—like to have things clear-cut. A police officer's job is to find evidence, to get to the bottom of things. Investigating ritual abuse cases, with people with DID as your witnesses, is a bizarre experience itself. These cases will end up on police records labelled as "unsolved", or deleted as a "no crime", because the allegation cannot be substantiated in any way. But that is no reason not to keep trying.

CHAPTER THREE

The Extreme Abuse Surveys: preliminary findings regarding dissociative identity disorder

Thorsten Becker, Wanda Karriker, Bettina Overkamp, & Carol Rutz

Where are the data?

Experts and sceptics in the field of dissociative disorders have, for at least 25 years, been asking the question: where are the data?[1] The preliminary results of three international online surveys (offered in English and German) are starting to show quantitative, as well as qualitative, data regarding the accounts of survivors of extreme abuse. Many of the survey participants had developed dissociative identity disorder when they were children, as a defence against the horrors of these crimes.

Ideologically motivated crimes

In his work as a case consultant with law-enforcement agencies in Europe, co-author Becker has coined and uses the term *ideologically motivated crimes* (IMC) to describe crimes that are committed in the name of and justified by a transcendent religious belief system (e.g. Aum Shin Rikyo: Lifton, 2000) or an immanent *Weltanschauung* (e.g. Nazi-ideology group). In the former, the physical presence of leaders and perpetrators is supported and/or enforced by gods or deities who are non-terrestrial beings and therefore can be perceived as omnipresent, especially by young children. This is a serious threat and may continue as a stressor to them even when they become adults. In the latter, a group's leadership exists in the temporal world, and rewards for suffering or committing criminal activities happen in their earthly lives.

Abusive rituals are often part of ceremonial practices designed to indoctrinate followers and condition or program them with the views, values, and ideology of the group.

Compounding the difficulties encountered by law enforcement when investigating IMC is the possibility that some of these crimes have occurred in staged settings (e.g. inside a UFO or submarine). Apparently these scenarios are intentionally designed to make the victims appear delusional when they recount their experiences in a forensic setting or even in the sanctity of a psychotherapist's office. Whether or not perpetrators stage events to exploit the bodies, minds, and souls of their victims, whether or not they hide behind a religious or non-religious ideology to justify and satisfy their perverse needs, the examination of these cases presents a challenge not limited to persons in the law-enforcement field.

Co-author Rutz has written and spoken extensively about another category of extreme abuse that can also be classified as IMC. In a lecture at Indiana University in 2003, she challenged her audience of criminal justice students: "The nature of my memories includes incest, ritual abuse, and government experimentation. How does one understand and talk about the horrors of growing up in an intergenerational cult, let alone being drafted into service by our government as a child guinea pig?" (Rutz, 2003).

In her book, *A Nation Betrayed: The Chilling True Story of Secret Cold War Experiments Performed on Our Children and Other Innocent People*, Rutz provides documentation that the types of horrific crimes she remembers were carried out in government-funded projects in the name of national security:

> On December 17, 1999 I turned 52 years old. On that day I received three CD ROMs from the CIA in response to my FOIA

request. Forty-eight years after I was first experimented on, I found solid proof of my memories—proof that was in the government vaults of the nearly 18,000 pages of declassified documents from the Bluebird/Artichoke and MKULTRA programs. One of the documents specifically stated that experimental studies of the postulated abilities of a few specially gifted subjects would be conducted [Subproject 136 of MKULTRA CIA Mori ID#17395 ESP Research, 1961 and 1962, declassified documents from CIA]. The document states, "that in working with individual subjects, special attention will be given to dissociative states which tend to accompany spontaneous ESP experiences. Such states can be induced and controlled to some extent with hypnosis and drugs. . . . The data used in the study will be obtained from special groups such as psychotics, children and mediums. . . ."

The document continues, "Learning studies will be instituted in which the subject will be rewarded or punished for his overall performance and reinforced in various ways by being told whether he was right, by being told what the target was, with electric shock etc." The proposal then goes on to say, "In other cases drugs and psychological tricks will be used to modify his attitudes. The experimenters will be particularly interested in dissociative states, from the abaissement de niveau mental, to multiple personality in so-called mediums; and an attempt will be made to induce a number of states of this kind, using hypnosis." The government had finally handed me the validation I had been searching for. To say my heart stopped that day is almost true. [Rutz, 2001, pp. xvii–xviii]

Although there might be no laws prohibiting what happens in secret experiments,[2] who could deny that the torture of a child "in the name of" national security is not an ideologically motivated crime—and a crime that is relevant to the theme of this book and the research data presented in this chapter?

Our survey data show that Rutz is not alone in remembering both satanic ritual abuse and traumatic mind-control procedures. But numbers cannot tell the whole story. Survivors can, as does this person who wrote to one of the authors:[3]

"I am proud that I survived incest, ritual abuse and government experimentation; however, the perpetrators should not be. What was done to me was ruthless, tragic, degrading, not to speak of illegal. My government to which I pay taxes needs to be accountable for what happened to me and other children who were tortured in concentration camp-like experiments. It is bad enough that such abuse happened to adults—but to unknowing children? It was not only criminal, but inhumane."

THE TRILOGY
The EAS, P–EAS, and C–EAS surveys

EAS: Extreme Abuse Survey for adult survivors

The EAS, an international online survey for adult survivors of extreme abuse, was conducted between 1 January and 30 March 2007.

On 31 December 2006, Rutz had sent an email announcement of the EAS to survivors and survivor advocates on her email lists, with this request:

> Forward this email announcement to other RA/MC survivors whom you know, email lists of survivors, and all professionals you know who work with survivors and ask them to forward to others and ask others to forward to survivors and to professionals including therapists, physicians, clergy, deprogrammers, researchers, law enforcement, attorneys and others who have worked with RA/MC survivors literally sending the announcement around the world.

The purpose of this survey was "to explore commonalities reported by survivors of extreme abuse including but not limited to ritual abuse and mind control [RA/MC]". Finding no consensus in the academic or survivor literature for a definition of these terms, we had decided to let the participants define these terms within their own frames of reference.

The EAS was viewed by 2,337 people: 1,719 in English, 618 in German. Of these, 1,471 people answered at least one of the 187 (and additional 53 optional) questions.

There were 31 countries named—United States 774, Germany 273, United Kingdom 92, Canada 75, Australia 38, Switzerland 13, Israel 11, Norway 10, Netherlands 8, Austria 8, New Zealand

6, South Africa 6, Greece 5, Sweden 4, Armenia 3, India 3, Spain 2, France 2, Colombia 2, Belgium 1, Bulgaria 1, Czech Republic 1, Ireland 1, Italy 1, Romania 1, China 1, Hong Kong 1, Kyrgyzstan 1, Mexico 1, Malaysia 1, Saudi Arabia 1—but 124 respondents did not name a country of residence.

A total of 1,190 respondents gave their primary languages—English 852, German 256, Dutch 21, Norwegian 10, Hebrew 6, French 6, Greek 5, Swedish 4, Italian 3, Spanish 3, Afrikaans 3, Polish 3, Turkish 2, Estonian 2, Tamil 2, Chinese Simplified 2, Romanian 1, Azerbaijani 1, Bengali 1, Georgian 1, Czech 1, Finnish 1, Korean 1, Persian 1, Armenian 1, Pashto 1—but 281 respondents did not name their primary languages.

In terms of demographics, 1,440 respondents gave their gender: 81% of these were female, 18% were male, and 1% were transgendered. Current age was given by 1,451 respondents, and 70% of these were under 50 years.

P–EAS: Professional–Extreme Abuse Survey

The P–EAS, an international online survey for therapists, counsellors, clergy, and other persons who have worked professionally with at least one adult survivor of extreme abuse, was conducted between 1 April and 30 June 2007.

A rationale posted on the opening page read:

> Ten years ago, the therapeutic community faced the first criminal trial involving charges against therapists in connection with "false" or "recovered" memories of ritual abuse (*US v Peterson, Seward, Mueck, Keraga and Davis* CR No H-97–237). Although charges were dismissed in March, 1999, the phenomenon of RA/MC remains a controversial issue among therapists, counselors, investigators, and the courts. Only a few empirical studies in peer-reviewed journals provide descriptive data reported by adult survivors regarding the types of ritual abuse they have experienced and its mental and physical sequelae. No studies involve interviews with survivors of mind control experimentation or professionals who have worked with them.

The P-EAS was viewed by 656 people: 458 in English, 198 in German. Of these, 451 persons answered at least one of the 215 (and additional 53 optional) questions.

There were 20 countries named—United States 205, Germany 99, United Kingdom 59, Canada 21, Netherlands 9, New Zealand 4, Switzerland 4, Norway 4, Israel 4, Australia 3, Greece 3, Ireland 2, Philippines 2, Belgium 1, Italy 1, Romania 1, Sweden 1, South Africa 1, Ecuador 1, Hungary 1—but 24 respondents did not name a country of residence.

A total of 389 respondents gave their primary languages— English 265, Germany 88, Dutch 18, Greek 4, Norwegian 4, Filipino 2, Spanish 2, Hebrew 2, Romanian 1, Hungarian 1, Italian 1, Swedish 1—but 62 respondents did not name their primary languages.

In terms of demographics, 438 respondents gave their gender: 84.5% of these were female, 15.5% were male, and 0% were transgendered. Current age was given by 444 respondents, and 57% of these were over 50 years.

C–EAS: Child–Extreme Abuse Survey

After a considerable number of requests to do another survey, this time focusing on children, the C–EAS, an international online survey for caregivers of child survivors of ritual abuse and mind control, was conducted between 8 July and 8 October 2007.

The C–EAS was developed for

> persons who have served as caregivers for children who have made disclosures consistent with ritual abuse and associated traumatic mind control procedures designed to ensure victims' loyalty to the perpetrators(s) or perpetrator groups.

Caregiver was defined as

> a person who has provided physical, psychological, medical, spiritual, legal, educational and/or other types of support to at least one child victim of RA/MC who was under 18 at the time the care was given.

We limited the C-EAS categories of abuse to RA/MC by stating:

> For purposes of this online questionnaire, the surveyors operationally define ritual abuse and mind control using the definition for "ritual violence" proposed by Becker and the German journalist and author of *Vater Unser in der Holle* [Our Father in Hell], Ulla Fröhling (1996):
>
>> Ritual Violence is a severe form of abuse of adults, adolescents and children intended to traumatize the victims. It consists of physical, sexual and psychological forms of abuse which are planned out and systematically used in ceremonies. These ceremonies may have an ideological background as well as being staged for the purpose of deception and threat. Symbols, activities or rituals which have religious, magical or supernatural connotations are used. The purpose is to confuse, threaten and terrorize victims as well as indoctrinate them with religious, spiritual or ideological beliefs. Ritual violence rarely consists of a single episode. Most often these experiences happen over an extended period of time.

The C–EAS was viewed by 395 people: 262 in English, 133 in German. Of these, 264 people answered at least one of the 260 questions.

There were 19 countries named—United States 116, Germany 67, United Kingdom 24, Canada 12, Armenia 4, New Zealand 3, France 2, Australia 2, Netherlands 2, Peru 1, Philippines 1, Poland 1, Portugal 1, Switzerland 1, Hungary 1, Israel 1, Turkey 1, Venezuela 1, South Africa 1—but 22 respondents did not name a country of residence.

A total of 222 respondents gave their primary languages—English 148, German 57, Dutch 6, Spanish 4, Faroese 1, Polish 1, Amharic 1, Hungarian 1, Armenian 1, Afrikaans 1, Frisian 1—but 42 respondents did not name their primary languages.

In terms of demographics, 257 respondents gave their gender: 83% of these were female, 15% were male, and 2% were transgendered. Current age was given by 262 respondents, and 68% of these were under 50 years.

Results

The surveys were analysed in terms of the following categories:

- dissociation and RA/MC
- ideologically motivated crimes addressed in the trilogy (RA and MC)
- ideological background of alleged perpetrator groups
- corroboration for RA/MC crimes
- legal responses to disclosures
- healing methods

Dissociation and RA/MC

Table 3.1 presents the number of people who responded to statements regarding dissociation and RA/MC, and the percentages of these who clicked on "n/a", "yes", "don't know" (d/k), or "no".

Of those who answered "yes" to the first question ("I have been diagnosed with DID"), 84% reported that they are survivors of RA/MC.

TABLE 3.1.   **Dissociation and RA/MC**

Statement	Survey	N	Responses (%)			
			n/a	yes	d/k	no
I have been diagnosed with DID.	EAS	1,007	2	65	5	27
The majority of adult RA/MC survivors with whom I have worked has met the diagnostic criteria for DID.	P-EAS	234	4	85	3	8
Child has DID as a possible after-effect of RA/MC.	C-EAS	83	1	74	18	7
Child dissociates when talking or questioned about abuse.	C-EAS	108	3	84	7	6

40 THORSTEN BECKER ET AL.

Ideologically motivated crimes addressed in the trilogy

Ritual abuse

If perpetrated in ritualistic settings, a sample of 10 identical items from both the EAS and P–EAS and 10 similar items from the C–EAS could be classified as ideologically motivated crimes. A statistical analysis of responses across surveys for these items was conducted using chi-square tests. The purpose of this procedure was to determine whether the distribution of "yes", "don't know", and "no" responses was the same for extreme-abuse survivors who reported each memory, professionals who have worked with at least one survivor reporting the memory, and caregivers of at least one child survivor of RA/MC who had made a verbal disclosure of the crime. Results indicate statistically significant differences among these groups in the frequencies of reports of these crimes (all $p < .01$).

Table 3.2 presents the total number (N) who responded to these items and the percent of "yes" responses, by each survey group. A comparison of these distributions suggests that the main difference in responses across groups is the higher percentages of "yes" responses by professionals. This is a reasonable conclusion given that the majority of P–EAS respondents report having worked with more than one survivor of RA/MC and thus would have more opportunities to hear reports of ideologically motivated crimes.

Table 3.3 presents the total number of persons who responded "yes" to statements on the EAS regarding ritual abuse, followed by the number from each area: United States (US), Canada (CA), Europe (EU), and other countries (Other).

Mind Control

Table 3.4 presents the total number of persons who responded "yes" to statements on the EAS regarding mind control, followed by the number from each area: United States (US), Canada (CA), Europe (EU), other countries (Other).

Of the 257 respondents who reported secret mind-control experiments used on them as children, 69% (177) reported having been abused in a satanic cult.

TABLE 3.2. Ideologically motivated crimes. Ritual abuse (all surveys)

Item	EAS		P-EAS		C-EAS	
	N	%	*N*	%	*N*	%
Receiving physical abuse from perpetrators	1,093	88	216	97	90	82
Sexual abuse by multiple perpetrators	1,090	82	217	95	91	77
Forced drugging	1,077	73	221	88	88	70
Witnessing murder by perpetrators	1,057	56	218	77	96	43
Forced to participate in animal mutilations/killings	1,059	55	218	78	92	59
Pornography (child)	1,059	55	220	82	83	53
Forced participation in murder by perpetrators	1,040	48	220	70	90	42
Prostitution (child)	1,045	48	218	77	79	25
Forced impregnation	1,041	40	220	71	82	33
Survivor's own child murdered by his/her perpetrators	1,021	26	217	55	82	18

TABLE 3.3. Ideologically motivated crimes. Ritual abuse (EAS only)

Statement	All	US	CA	EU	Other
I was ritually abused in a satanic cult.	543	360	33	97	53
I have watched a person being flayed.	307	201	21	43	32
I was ritually abused in a Fascist group.	215	149	17	31	18
Perpetrators have on at least one occasion made me believe that external entities/spirits/demons had taken over my body.	530	311	32	124	63

TABLE **3.4.** **Ideologically motivated crimes. Mind control (EAS only)**

Statement	All	US	CA	EU	Other
Secret government-sponsored mind-control experiments were performed on me as a child.	257	185	25	27	20
My perpetrator(s) deliberately created/programmed dissociative states of mind (such as alters, personalities, ego-states) in me.	640	391	42	136	61
I have experienced mind-control programming through which I was trained to become an assassin.	175	128	16	13	18
I remember being used in government-sponsored mind-control experiments in a country other than the U.S. or Canada.	127	89	5	22	21

Ideological background of alleged perpetrator groups

C–EAS

Table 3.5 presents the number of caregivers who reported on the C–EAS that the child or children under their care had mentioned an alleged perpetrator group. Between 62 and 87 people responded.

P-EAS

Respondents on the P–EAS were asked to report the approximate number of their adult clients who had reported memories consistent with the abuses/tortures listed. The responses are presented in Table 3.6 (e.g. 20 respondents reported no satanic ritual abuse clients; 56 reported 1; 74 reported between 2 and 10; 28 reported between 11 and 20; and 41 reported more than 20).

TABLE 3.5.   Ideological background of alleged perpetrator groups:
C–EAS

Alleged perpetrator group	N
Brujeria	0
Child pornography	43
Child trafficking	23
Day-care employees	18
Fascist group (e.g. Neo-Nazi, White Supremacist, KKK, or any other group that considers itself superior in race, creed, or origin)	22
Fraternal organizations	19
Gnostic-occult	18
Government-sponsored mind-control "experimenters"	13
Juvenile satanic groups	11
Mainstream religious groups	22
Non-government-sponsored mind-control "experimenters"	16
Organized crime group	22
Organized paedophile group	35
Palo Mayombe	0
Polygamous groups	6
Private school employees	8
Public school employees	16
Religious sect (a group made up of dissenters from an established faith such as a Christian sect)	19
Santeria	1
Satanic cult	55
Unnamed group without a remarkable ideology	25
Vampirism	10
Voodoo	7
Witchcraft	30
Other	10

TABLE 3.6.   Ideological background of alleged perpetrator groups: P–EAS

Statement	0	1	2–10	11–20	20+
Ritual abuse in a satanic cult.	20	56	74	28	41
Ritual abuse in a Gnostic-occult group.	88	31	31	5	10
Ritual abuse in a child pornography group.	39	58	67	13	32
Ritual abuse in a traditional religious group.	78	39	58	12	22
Ritual abuse in a religious sect.	84	37	42	4	13
Ritual abuse in a Fascist group.	112	31	31	0	13
Ritual abuse in an unnamed group without a remarkable ideology.	86	34	50	5	14
Ritual abuse in a named group other than those listed.	101	22	20	2	9
Having been trafficked as a child.	49	57	65	16	24
Having been trafficked as an adult.	91	30	51	10	10
Having been a child victim of state-sponsored torture.	118	17	33	5	11
Having been an adult victim of state-sponsored torture.	125	23	21	7	9
Having been a child victim of torture that was not state-sponsored.	29	43	79	17	36
Having been an adult victim of torture that was not state-sponsored.	83	30	40	9	22
Having been an adult victim of torture that was not state-sponsored.	120	21	32	7	6
Having been a subject of government-sponsored mind-control experimentation as a child.	113	23	31	10	9
Having been a subject of government-sponsored mind-control experimentation as an adult.	130	17	16	6	6
Ritual abuse by clergy.	67	50	59	9	19
Ritual abuse in a polygamist group.	126	15	23	5	3

Corroboration for RA/MC crimes

Tables 3.7 and 3.8 present the number of people who responded on the EAS and the P–EAS, respectively, to statements regarding corroboration for RA/MC crimes, and the percentages of these who clicked on "n/a", "yes", "don't know" (d/k), or "no".

TABLE 3.7.   Corroboration for RA/MC crimes: EAS

		Responses (%)			
Statement	N	n/a	yes	d/k	no
At least one of my perpetrators has been convicted of criminal abuse towards me.	992	3	7	9	81
I have heard other survivors, whom I had not previously met, describe the same perpetrators of my own abuse.	986	3	34	7	56
I have heard other survivors, whom I had not previously met, describe the same places where I was abused.	978	3	32	6	59
I have successfully sued my perpetrator(s) in civil court.	964	3	2	1	95
Current access by RA/MC perpetrators involves harm to my physical/mental/spiritual well-being.	1,002	6	34	14	45

TABLE 3.8.   Corroboration for RA/MC crimes: P–EAS

		Responses (%)			
Statement	N	n/a	yes	d/k	no
I have heard two or more adult RA/MC survivors name the same perpetrator(s).	230	4	35	4	57
I have heard two or more adult RA/MC survivors name the same place(s) of abuse.	231	4	40	4	52
I have been harmed by an alleged RA/MC perpetrator or perpetrator group in apparent retaliation for working professionally with one of their victims.	227	4	10	7	80
I have worked with at least one adult survivor of RA/MC who has successfully sued his/her perpetrator(s) in civil court.	222	3	08	4	86

Tables 3.9 presents the number of people on the C–EAS who responded to statements regarding corroboration for RA/MC crimes, and the percentages of these who clicked on "n/a", "yes", or "no".

Legal responses to disclosures (C–EAS)

Tables 3.10 presents the number of people on the C–EAS who responded to statements regarding legal responses to disclosure, and the percentages of these who clicked on "n/a", "yes", or "no".

TABLE 3.9.   Corroboration for RA/MC crimes: C–EAS

Statement	N	Responses (%)		
		n/a	yes	no
Affirmative legal outcomes for one or more perpetrators.	80	1	31	68
Confession of one or more perpetrators.	80	3	24	74
Discovery of ritual paraphernalia mentioned by one or more children.	78	3	22	76
Discovery of ritual sites mentioned by one or more children.	80	4	31	65
Medical evidence consistent with RA/MC.	80	3	53	45
Photographs depicting RA/MC on the child or children under your care.	76	4	08	88
Psychological symptoms consistent with RA/MC.	88	3	91	07
Ritual wounds; scarring on or around genitals.	77	3	40	57
Ritual wounds; scarring on parts of body not including genital area.	76	3	46	51
Symptoms abate when child is given opportunity to talk about the abuse, to tell the story.	78	3	64	33
Two or more children independently reporting same perpetrator(s).	83	2	52	46
Videos depicting RA/MC on the child or children under your care.	78	4	12	85

TABLE 3.10.   Legal responses to disclosures: C–EAS

Statement	N	Responses (%)		
		n/a	yes	no
I have reported the RA/MC of one or more children under my care to social services.	83	6	55	39
Social services have substantiated one of more of my reports.	79	10	25	65
Social services have determined one or more of my reports to be unfounded.	80	13	25	63
I have reported the RA/MC of one or more children under my care to law enforcement.	84	7	48	45
At least one perpetrator has been arrested.	82	4	27	70
Charges have been dismissed against at least one perpetrator.	76	9	40	51
At least one perpetrator has submitted a plea bargain.	76	9	15	76
At least one perpetrator has gone to trial.	77	7	22	71
At least one perpetrator has been convicted.	78	6	21	73
The verdict of at least one perpetrator who was convicted has been reversed.	75	11	05	84
At least one perpetrator has been sued in civil court.	76	8	12	80
At least one perpetrator has paid damages.	77	8	04	88

Healing methods (EAS)

Of 53 choices, the 10 healing methods ranked most effective (marked "help" or "great help") on the EAS by 655 of the respondents with DID were individual psychotherapy/counselling, creative writing, supportive friends, journaling, art therapy, personal prayer/meditation, abreactive work, drawing/painting, formal deprogramming, and grounding techniques (Karriker, 2007).

CONCLUDING COMMENTS

The purpose of this chapter is to share preliminary data from the Extreme Abuse Surveys relevant to the forensic aspects of DID. Selecting the specific data to present turned out to be quite a challenge. We could argue that every bit of over a half million pieces of data generated from the massive response to our online surveys is relevant to the topic. All of our respondents—adult survivors, their helpers/healers who hold their pain, the child caregivers—have been touched, tormented, and terrorized by crimes so unimaginable that professionals cannot even agree on a name for them.

As developers of the survey, we did not anticipate that results would point out how limiting are the terms "ritual abuse", "sadistic abuse", or "satanic ritual abuse" as used in the professional literature or even by survivors themselves. These words do not justify the horror of the crimes or debilitating after-effects of the atrocities that respondents have reported. The "ritual" connotation fails to encompass many of the tortures, threats, confinements, mind-control procedures, violence, and other types of unlawful or immoral exploitation that participants have endured.

It is clear that many of the crimes that survivors suffered were perpetrated in the name of some greater good or evil (as perceived by secular perpetrator groups) or greater god or devil (as perceived by "religious" perpetrator groups). As opposed to criminals who operate without an ideological motivation, typically these perpetrators appear dedicated to doing the right thing in service to their belief systems. In German this is called *Ueberzeugungstaeter*. Consequently, there is little chance for re-socialization or rehabilitation for ideological criminals. According to Becker's terminology, their crimes could be classified as ideologically motivated crimes.

IMC represent a further challenge to the thinking processes of survivors and professionals alike. Accepting IMC into one's world view requires a broadening of the concepts of RA/MC. Pertinent to this discussion is the ongoing threat of violent and mass-murdering forms of terrorism committed in the name of a religion. Terrorists and RA/MC perpetrators appear to share much in common with respect to their needs for gratification from and justification for their crimes against humanity. Perhaps they also share the same capacity for "doubling"—living two parallel, seemingly independent lives, as described by Lifton (1986).

The concept of doubling as a type of dissociation is worthy of investigation if one is interested in understanding the so-called sleeper agents or the lives of Islamic terrorists within a Western society during training (such as the pilots of 9/11 in Hamburg, Germany).

To our knowledge, these phenomena have not been researched. It might be crucial for the prevention of terroristic acts to develop an understanding of IMC and related dissociative disorders.

Victims of mass terrorism—and potential victims (that is, all of us), if hit with these acts—would likely defend with the same traumatic responses, including various degrees of dissociation, as do other survivors of extreme abuse.

We sincerely hope that the success of our preliminary effort to reach survivors, therapists, helpers/healers, and caregivers will encourage further research and educational training about the relationships between IMC, DID, and forensics.

Notes

1. The United Nations Commission on Human Rights (2002) "invites States and interested NGOs to undertake research with a view to achieving a better understanding of the misuse of some ritual practices to intimidate women and girl victims of trafficking."

2. But Louisiana Statute #107.1, *Ritualistic Acts*, states: "The provisions of this Section shall not be construed to apply to any state or federally approved, licensed, or funded research project" (Louisiana Statutes, 1989).

3. Quoted in Rutz & Karriker (2008), *Government-Funded Mind Control/ Medical Experimentation (Quotes to Ponder)*.

CHAPTER FOUR

The protectors of the secrets

"Aahbee"

I am a female survivor of childhood neglect, trauma, and abuse, now in middle age. I have dissociative identity disorder and am on a therapy-based journey of recovery. In sharing from my own experience, I am aiming to avoid graphic details but, instead, to reflect on the impact of various deprivations, traumatic occurrences, and abuses on the development of a number of distinct parts to my persona.

Dissociation is a survival strategy that enables one to tolerate the intolerable and survive the catastrophic. In a dysfunctional and traumatic home environment, an outward appearance of normality must be maintained in order to avoid aggravating the abuser. Imagine a lake, the quiet surface representing daily life and consciousness. When overwhelmingly painful traumas occur, threatening to disturb the surface, dissociation separates and contains the memories and emotions, as if in a bubble or balloon, which is then weighted down out of sight on the bed of the lake, far away from consciousness. Daily life goes on, the secrets of both the abuser and the abused protected.

By adulthood I had twelve such "balloons" on my lakebed, each still chock-full of unbearable pain and horror, some of them revisiting the surface when circumstances required, some of them later bursting up unannounced and catching the adult me off guard. How did these parts, or "balloons", come to be formed in the first place?

My two older brothers were much of the way through primary school when my father raped his wife, and my twin sister and I were conceived. This was a vengeful act by a cruel man who never wanted to be a father. My chronically abused mother was recovering from a psychotic breakdown and was hoping to leave him and return to her parents, but a further pregnancy bound her to him for many more years. She would only have been welcome back to her parents' home as an unpaid maid without the encumbrance of children.

My mother was advised to have a termination on medical grounds due to her severe grand-mal epilepsy, plus other medical conditions that made pregnancy dangerous for her, but she refused. Imagine her mixed feelings when my twin sister died and was miscarried. My persistence was initially unknown of, my enlarging presence unwelcome. Throughout the remaining pregnancy my father verbally and physically abused my mother and brothers. Between bouts of infidelity he also sexually abused my mother. Her physical and mental health deteriorated, culminating in a near-fatal epileptic seizure during my delivery at home, while I was trapped with the umbilical cord bound tightly round my neck. I breathed once released, so I was promptly put in the corner while the lone midwife fought to keep Mummy alive. It was some time before she could hold me and feed me. My Daddy, Mummy, and Nan were all variously mentally and physically unwell, rendering them unwilling and/or unable to meet my early needs.

I cannot remember a time without a profound underlying sense of isolation, badness, guilt, and shame. I still struggle with recurrent anxiety that I am responsible for others being unwell and need to make them feel better. I may wrestle cognitively and logically with the nonsense that this represents to my adult thinking, but these beliefs and feelings pre-date rational thought and are largely resistant to change. It is as if they are the foundations on which the rest of my psyche was rather unsteadily built.

For my first five years I slept in a cot in my parents' bedroom. Unspeakable things went on there at times, sometimes involving just my Daddy and Mummy, and sometimes me too. When the pain, terror, and helplessness became overwhelming, a part of me that I will call Tiny took over, while I escaped by floating out of the window, to a peaceful sunlit garden, until it was safe enough to return to the cot. Tiny's memories and feelings were kept entirely separate from the smiling, good little girl I will call Daytimer who appears in the handful of photos that remain from that time. Many years later Tiny wrote, with my hand but in squiggly child-like writing, "my Daddy is hurting my Mummy again and i can't stop him. If i cry he hurts her and me, if i go to the garden he hurts her. If she dies i die. i just have to lie really really quiet and still and see if am dead later."

I still feel intense pain that Mummy just lay there while Daddy used me. She was, I guess, petrified with fear herself, yet this invasion by one parent not mitigated in any way by the other was an extremely potent message that I was on my own, worth neither protecting nor fighting for, just someone else's toy.

Daytimer tried to be good and smiley so Mummy wouldn't cry and Daddy wouldn't shout, but she was never good enough or smiley enough to stop bad things happening. When Daddy put his hat on and went out of the house in the morning, he was nice to people and didn't shout and hurt them. Daytimer thought she was a very bad girl because when he came home Daddy shouted and hurt us, especially if he'd been to that pub place and smelt of smoke and beer.

Horrors could also happen in broad daylight, especially if Mummy had run away. The warning signs were around getting told off, which remains a very powerful trigger to this day. I remember being told off, told off, told off and Daddy saying "Come here ya little bugger" before dragging me by my hair into the shed. Another part I'll call Little Bugger took over, but she was very naughty and was sick down him, so he slapped her head from side to side until she stood still. I floated by Daddy's right-hand side, watching what was happening but not part of it. The memories have no sound, just a slow-motion, rather blurry playback of abhorrent things happening to a very small girl who looks rather like Daytimer did at that age. Little Bugger still believes that she is a very evil little girl for Daddy to punish her like that. She kept her secrets well, far away from the rest of us, way down on the "lake bed", for decades.

Daytimer was learning, even before school age, to hide and conceal things that might make Mummy cry or get Daddy angry. Whenever there was a knock at the door, Mummy and I froze in fear and had to put smiley faces on and say nothing, otherwise even worse things might happen after the people left. So when the two big men with hats came [an NSPCC inspector and a policeman], Daytimer sat very quietly in the corner and smiled, just like Mummy. They wanted to know how my brothers kept bruising themselves so badly. Daytimer didn't have many bruises so they didn't ask her if she was alright, but even if they had she probably would have smiled and nodded and said "Yes thank you."

Daddy had something called a breakdown after that and was taken away to hospital. We lost our money and our house and were supposed to be sad, but actually it was much nicer when Daddy was away, especially when it was just Mummy and me, because she smiled sometimes.

I didn't start primary school until I was nearly 6, but I was quick-learning and advanced, partly because my ambitious father had given me regular homework beforehand so that I wouldn't show him up. At last there was something I was good at, and I enjoyed learning new things. I wanted to please Daddy and my teacher. I didn't understand that Daddy was never going to be pleased, no matter what, but I kept on trying, hoping that one day he might be proud of me. That hope resisted all reason and logic and only finally died when he did, 40 years later.

Being so bound up inside by fear is very lonely. I'm aware of many inhibitory messages from that stage: don't make Daddy angry; don't upset Mummy in case she has a fit; don't shout; don't cry; don't run to Daddy if you fall and hurt yourself; keep very quiet and still in bed and don't call out for help; don't go to Mummy and Daddy's room if you have a nightmare, there may be a worse one really happening there; don't ever tell anybody what happens when Daddy gets drunk or angry, even if they are your teacher or Daddy's doctor or psychiatrist or from the NSPCC or the police, because Mummy might die. The simultaneous imperatives made it all very confusing; you must always be good, polite, obedient, and happy-looking; always tell the truth and not lies; work very hard at school and act as if everything is all right.

The only memory I have of an adult asking my opinion is ghastly. While I was between the ages of 5 and 10, Daddy was in and out of mental hospital with psychotic depression. The old hospital had once been a workhouse. It had a very peculiar smell to it and scary men wandering around, some of them twitching and jerking as they moved along. I now understand that they were suffering side-effects from the antipsychotic medication, but at the time I thought they were having fits or trying to wink and leer at me. During one visit Mummy and I were taken into a room where Daddy and his psychiatrist were waiting. I had very little idea of what was going on and was frightened stiff of both men. The psychiatrist suddenly turned to me and said: "Well, little girl, I'm sure you want your Daddy home, don't you." It wasn't a question, so I looked up with eyes wide as saucers and nodded, having absolutely no idea that my response meant anything. Mummy was very easily upset but rarely openly angry. On that two-hour bus journey home, I was left in no doubt that it was my fault that Daddy was on his way home to hurt us all again.

One fine summer's day, at the age of 7, I was entrusted to the care of some older children to go paddling and fishing in a nearby stream. Afterwards they didn't take me home but to some woods. What one of them tried to do, while the others held me down, should never happen to anyone. A part of me I'll call Seven took over while I floated up in the air and looked back down on the scene. I remember her with clothes on even though she must have been naked. I believed their threats to kill me if my parents found out, and I kept silent for a year before accidentally letting out a clue in the middle of a family fight. Interrogation, humiliation, and accusation followed. Mummy wailed and sobbed, saying, "My little girl is ruined for ever"; Daddy just stared into space and said nothing. Other reactions and consequences followed, including a very traumatic medical examination. No one comforted the little girl or said it wasn't her fault. All this confirmed that we were on our own, whatever terrible things were yet to come, any hope of carefree childhood over.

Around this time Daytimer developed very protective feelings towards our epileptic Mummy. When a violent fight broke out, she had to stay and make sure that Mummy didn't choke during a fit. She watched from the side of the room, frozen with fear. Then if Mummy did fall down, stop breathing, and start jerking, it was almost as if a Little Nurse person, of about my height, stepped out of me and went to help Mummy. She would roll Mummy on her side, take her false teeth out, and stop her banging her head on any furniture until the seizure stopped. It must have been me that moved, but somehow having part of me stay watching and only a part of me step in to the middle of the fight was less scary.

I was also beginning to realize that not all families were like ours—not questioning or comparing yet, but just noticing a few things. Some mummies weren't too frightened to go outside in the daytime and even went to the village shop instead of sending their little girls. Some daddies didn't shout and hit people, even behind the closed doors of their own home, or take too many tablets and get taken away to hospital. Some mummies didn't disappear for days at a time when the daddies returned home. It would never have crossed my mind to complain or ask for help or tell anyone outside the home. In fact, it all had be kept a really big secret, otherwise terrible things would happen and Mummy might die.

The need to protect the secrets was confirmed beyond question when my brother finally got tall enough to fight Daddy back and try to help Mummy. My brother was taken away by the police and didn't come home again for two years. In all that time, not a single person visited him.

So Mummy and Daytimer tried to be as good as possible so that Daddy didn't get angry and then things might be all right for a while. Of course, he might get drunk at the pub or lose on the horses and be very angry and hurt us anyway, but there was nothing anyone could do about that. Mummy modelled being a doormat, a powerless, compliant victim, and my job was to be a good girl like Mummy and try to please Daddy.

Both parents taught us to wear masks of normality when we left the house. Life was a series of role-plays. So there was Daytimer for home, a part that went to school, and a part that sometimes went out to play, but always underlain by a gnawing sense of isolation, of watching life happen to other people while worrying about what was happening at home.

Thankfully, Daytimer didn't know Tiny, Little Bugger, or Seven, because each of them, on their own, knew more than was bearable. Their memories and feelings were completely separate. The intensity and tensions of everyday life were awful, and other strategies helped me get by. I played elaborate imaginary games with dolls in my bedroom, or escaped on my little bike to ride around the countryside where I could sing to myself and daydream of happy endings.

Some twists and turns of fate seem particularly harsh. My little bike broke, and there was no one at home to help. So I wheeled it to a man in the village who mended things, with no idea that it was a very dangerous place for little girls where two men were waiting. Daytimer already knew the extra man, who didn't do the mending, was bad, because he had trapped and frozen her and done frightening things before. A part of me I'll call Geraldine survived that day. I put a different face on the girl and floated at the back of the room until it was over. Somehow we got ourselves home, with the still-broken bike and a made-up story about falling out of a tree to explain the bleeding.

Night-time was never restful in our house. During junior-school years, a part of me I'll call Francine dealt with abuse by Daddy. A kind of switch flicked inside when the warning signs reached red alert—floorboards creaking on the landing; the door beginning to move; shadows lengthening up the wall; the vivid stench of cigarette smoke and half-digested beer; time to "jump ship" or die. Pain of that intensity while your mouth is firmly covered and the breath is crushed out of your chest isn't just about invasion, it feels life-threatening and cannot be endured without some means of distancing and separation of the rest of life from it. On one occasion, when Daytimer was left injured with a marked limp, she made up a story that she was a very naughty girl with another name who was just pretending to limp to upset Mummy. Francine still believes that Daddy was trying to kill her, and if she'd been a good girl she would have stopped breathing and died.

I didn't understand why Mummy started sleeping on a mattress, blocking my bedroom door shut. One fateful night I woke up absolutely bursting to go for a wee-wee. Mummy pleaded with me to wait until morning but I just couldn't. I tiptoed as quiet as a mouse across the landing, past their bedroom door, to the bathroom. When I got back my bedroom door was blocked shut. Daddy had got in while I was out and was hurting Mummy. It was all my fault. Next day I found a plastic toy to wee in so I never had to go to the bathroom in the night again and hurt Mummy.

Mummy sometimes ran away from Daddy and disappeared for days at a time. Without a phone or car we just had to wait until she came back. The police weren't called, I guess in case Mummy told them what Daddy had done to make her leave. Years later I discovered that she had found refuge in a convent and returned there from time to time when life was unbearable for her.

My Daddy visited the pub most evenings, getting variously drunk depending on how much money he had left after buying his cigarettes and betting on the horses. Sometimes when Mummy ran away I was taken to the pub and put to bed upstairs there, so that Daddy could still have his beer. I don't think Daddy had any idea that I was sold in that bedroom for 2s6d, half a crown—or 12½ pence in new money. A part of me I'll call Pauline was gagged and bound, endured searing pain, and was used as a toy. The men said they would come to our house in the night and murder us if the secret got out, so she was completely shut away from the rest of us, with no one to talk to.

Around the age of 9 or 10 a part of me I'll call Rescuer no longer stood frozen at the side and watched Daddy commit crimes against Mummy. She had to be different from the other parts and not so frightened of Daddy. On one occasion, when a bitter argument was under way and violence seemed imminent, Rescuer rode her little bike several miles at a frantic pace to the house of Mummy's friend. Breathlessly Rescuer asked her to come and stop Daddy hurting Mummy, so Mummy's friend put the bike in her car boot and we sped back. Like most bullies Daddy was a coward and immediately shrank into a trembling, tearful little man who wouldn't hurt a fly. After she left, both my parents were very angry with Rescuer because she had called in someone from outside. Nearer by were neighbours, the post office, village shop, school and church, and yet no one could help: our family secrets had to be protected at all costs, to stop even worse things happening.

If I heard raised voices after bedtime, I would crouch part-way down the stairs and listen. One night, peeping through the banister, I saw Mummy leaning backwards through the open living-room window. Daddy's hands were tightly gripped round her neck, and her face was that strange purply colour it sometimes went during a fit. Rescuer ran down shouting and pulled him off her. Mummy said she had been trying to escape from him through the window, Daddy said he was trying to stop her from falling out of the window and hurting herself. Who was looking after who? So many things were confusing and difficult.

My closest shave with personal criminal intent was at around this time, and I still shudder at the thought. With my Mummy's phobia of walking through our village and no car, the weekly shop involved a long trek to town and back. At least five times that I can remember we returned to find a suicide note from Daddy on the kitchen cabinet. The fifth time Mummy had taken me for fish and chips in town as a special treat, meaning we were later back than Daddy expected. We saw the note, dropped the shopping, and ran upstairs. Unlike the previous times, where he had been sleepy but able to ask for an ambulance, this time he had rolled onto his back and swallowed his tongue. His breathing had stopped, and his face was that purply colour. Mummy and I caught each other's eyes, just for a few seconds, which are etched forever in my memory. Here lay our mean, sadistic, violent, drunken abuser within moments of death at his own hands. Should we wake the sleeping tiger so that he could maul us all again and again?

Yes, of course we did—he was a human being whose life was in mortal danger. Without exchanging a word, she rolled him on his side and opened his airway, while I ran to the phone box and dialled 999. Am I glad we saved his life? For the sake of our own sanity and humanity, yes I am. The fact that leaving him to die even crossed our minds is guilt-laden enough. For the sake of the ten more years she stayed with him, then no, of course not, but that wasn't a solution that either of us could have borne.

How could all this and more have happened to one little girl, before the age of 10? There are moments when I would rather be considered crazy or deceitful than acknowledge this as my own history. The emotional, physical, spiritual, and relational burdens of acknowledging and working through the myriad consequences, intrusive symptoms, and hindrances to normal life that result from such a beginning are hard to bear.

So much of childhood trauma, perhaps particularly when it

begins with one's attachment figures, leaves one feeling worthless, powerless, voiceless, and vulnerably isolated at an intensity that is hard to convey in words. Yet one learns to be anxious and hyper-alert without necessarily learning to protect oneself, because the memories are too separate from consciousness to be truly useful. As a teenager I was strangely naive and prone to overlooking gross character flaws in suitors and tutors alike. A pervading dread through adolescence was that I would somehow walk into a room containing all the people that knew me. Which role should I play? How should I act? They would all find out that I was just a shop front with nothing of value behind it.

If dissociation works so well in childhood, why don't the parts just stay separate and out of sight on the lake bed forever? It's true that continuing to rely on dissociation in adult life can be very disruptive to normal functioning. If an adult "floats away", "zones out", or "jumps ship" to cope with overwhelming feelings, per-haps while responsible for the well-being of children, workmates, or clients, his or her sense of time, place, and person can be greatly disturbed, with serious consequences.

In my case, it is almost as if these survival mechanisms had a sell-by date. Maybe survivors of neglect, trauma, and abuse, battling with insecure attachments, self-doubt, and poor self-es-teem, have low levels in their "lakes" in the first place. Perhaps the stresses of adult life drain the lake still further, bringing the "balloons" nearer the surface, making them harder to hold under water. Then triggering reminders, losses, and traumas mean they suddenly surface, bursting their long-held memories and feelings all over the calm-looking waters.

I battled with long-term insecurity, anxiety, and occasional mystifying bouts of overwhelming despair but kept pushing my-self on through training, career, marriage, and parenthood, ignor-ing my own needs. The long-term anxiety was aggravated into depression when my Mum died in my late thirties. She was the vulnerable one whom I had taken away from Dad, protected, and cared for. Why was facing Dad alone, with her dead, so much more scary? The long-held dissociative barriers began to crack, flashbacks began to intrude, and the battles with overwhelming feelings became more frequent. Willpower just wasn't enough to contain it all.

When the depression became severe and protracted, I went to a psychiatrist to get treatment. Thankfully he heard and understood and arranged for me to begin therapy. A year later my Dad died, and one of the other abusers turned up at his funeral. Many of the remaining dissociative barriers crumbled and fell, with triggers, flashbacks, and times of agonizing connection with various of my long-hidden "parts" that each held more pain than was bearable at the time. It was quite literally like falling to pieces. The help I received was life-saving. Now, three years later, the rebuilding and life-saving work goes on.

I have found returning memories to have an awful relief attached to them. Perhaps over days or weeks, triggering reminders, words, phrases, images, or smells begin to build up into something one would rather not recognize, like feeling profoundly nauseous. Finally one vomits up; the images of horror take shape. Yet the "vomit" cannot be flushed away but has to be incorporated as part of one's own history and narrative before the power of it to disrupt and destroy can finally be broken.

My adult perspective on my "bad, mad, and sad" Dad doesn't altogether cover the remaining questions and self-doubts, and, depending on my frame of mind, perceived warning signs of "bad things ahead" can still cause a rush of heart-fluttering, sweating, and frozen panic while I attempt to "re-group" internally and gather my present-day bearings. Some years ago, while physically fixed to a hospital bed after a major operation, I had to request a change of procedure as the night nurse repeatedly creaking my door open and peering in at me, lit only by a small bulb from outside the room, was setting off depth charges of distress and flashbacks to Francine. Thankfully I was heard and understood, and my requests were met on that occasion, not something that often happens when one has illogical, if not bizarre-sounding, triggers and symptoms.

You may ask which of the "balloons" contained the real me? Well, any of them and all of them—that's the work of therapy, to help me acknowledge, accept, connect, comfort, and contain all those various parts of me and hopefully, over time, join all of us seamlessly together at last into a complete person. Therapy is hard work and is complicated by real-time events and traumas. I was impatient to "get it all out and sort it" and to set the world record for the shortest time in therapy. Bad idea. Slow and steady works more quickly in the end than a re-traumatizing roller-coaster ride between being completely off-the-scale overwhelmed and moribund with numb amnesia.

Professional and survivor opinions vary greatly as to whether full integration of all the fragmented parts should be the eventual goal, or whether stable coexistence may sometimes be preferable. Personally I am hoping to be enabled to take on board all of my "little ones" in time. They have each suffered and borne a great deal, but they have gifts and skills too, "treasures of the darkness" if you will, which I am a lesser person without. Things look pretty hopeful here, most of the time—but come back in a few years and ask me how it works out.

I once asked my psychiatrist if there was any way, other than long-term therapy, to deal with all of this. He told me that I could probably survive adult life on long-term antidepressants, with periodic hospital admissions at times of particular stress; however, if I wanted to freely and fully enjoy life, then there was no way around the pain other than to walk right through the middle and out the other side.

As to the perpetrators, dissociation covers their tracks incredibly well. Even if my story is now believed, then what use is evidence 30 or 40 years old, remembered piecemeal over several years? The final agonizing twist of the knife is that in the very process of surviving by protecting the secrets, I may have allowed other little ones to come to harm from those abusers.

I write in the hope that by explaining—even in part—my own journey, others may gain insight and understanding into the protectors of the secrets within, so that together we can learn how to expose the devious perpetrators, prevent harm being done to other little ones, and assist survivors in finding relief and peace.

CHAPTER FIVE

Am I safe yet?

Sue Cross, with "Louise" (and her alters)

> "We were not the normal bag: an affable, funny teenager and
> then with the next breath we could have pinned you to the
> wall. We became hard, we fought, we were cocky, vulnerable,
> easy-going, funny, affable, dangerous, known to be bordering
> on evil, very bright, very thick, whatever we needed to be, and
> there was one thing we agreed on—we had to stay alive."
>
> HJ

Louise's story

L ife became so unbearable at home that when I was about 16
I ran away and lived on the streets. It was like being freed:
no rules or regulations, no bedtime, no going to school, and
I could do what I wanted when I wanted. There was a naivety
about me. I never thought of the consequences. I wasn't innocent,
but it was all a game, not serious, just fun and exciting, and I don't
think I deliberately did anything to hurt anybody.

Sometimes it was confusing. I'd be asleep, and the next thing I
was being woken up by a policeman and taken to hospital because

they said I'd taken an overdose. Once I got put in a children's home.

I met this girl. Liverpool was playing that afternoon at Wembley, but we had no money. I didn't think in a callous way: "I'm going to mug somebody." It was very immature, a naivety about it, but exciting, fun, and daring. We saw two girls in the park and asked for money. When they refused I remember saying, "If you don't give me some money I'll hit you," but thinking, "I don't want to hit them." I knew it was wrong, but I never realized how wrong. It felt like a playground spat. I never understood the severity of the crime; it was always a game, just mucking around. I had a Swiss army knife in my pocket and I remember thinking, "This will be a crack." I pulled it out and said, "If you don't give us any money we're going to get you." What happened was always "shaded" in my head.

The next thing I knew I was standing over a girl on the floor. I didn't remember doing anything, and we just walked off without any money. We saw a bloke, and I held the knife up to him. I remember him looking scared. The next thing I knew we heard sirens, and a police car stopped. I was so not bothered that I let them walk over to me. The police said, "You're nicked." In the police car I remember hearing myself being quite cocky, but that wasn't how I felt. I felt out of control all of a sudden.

When I got to the police station they charged me with assault, ABH, carrying an offensive weapon, and attempted robbery. They questioned me about beating up the girl and threatening her with the knife. They told me I'd hit her. I didn't remember, but there was no way I was going to admit that because they'd think I was a nutter or lying, so I admitted to doing it—it was easier. I was patching my story up to make sense of it. I coughed for the lot.

When they put me in the cells I just cried and cried. I was petrified. I hated being in the cells; it was dim and dismal. I felt trapped like there was no way out, like I'd been in that atmosphere of being trapped before.

I went to court the next morning. I was put in the van, and other girls got in. I was petrified and out of my depth. They scared the living daylights out of me. The police had said I'd probably be remanded in custody, and I remember thinking that the last thing I want to do is go to prison.

In court I was shaking. Due to the law at that time, as I was arrested with a 17-year-old, I appeared in a magistrates' court. The magistrate bailed me to a children's home. I then heard myself saying, "If you put me in a f_____ kid's home, I'll run away." In my head I was screaming, "What the f___ are you doing, Louise? Shut your mouth."

He said, "You give me no option but to remand you in Holloway for a week." I think the plan was to bring me back and put me in a children's home. In the cells I was terrified. I remember thinking, "What have I done, why have I done that?" As I was taken to Holloway, I was shaking. I was only 16.

I remember being in reception, and the next thing I was aware of was being taken onto the wing. The noise hit me, like a crescendo of voices behind closed doors, young, old, gruff, aggressive, very meek, but all mumbled in together and really confusing. I saw the nets and I thought that they'd be good to trampoline on, not realizing they were suicide nets. Then I saw the girls. Every one looked as if they could kill me, and I thought, "Oh shit, I am so dead." I don't remember going up to the cell, but I heard the officer tell me it was where I'd be staying and a girl saying, "My name's Billy and I'm a lesbian." She was extremely butch-looking, and I remember thinking, "Shit, I don't stand a chance." The next thing I was aware of was prison officers bursting in and a fire. I don't remember setting the fire. Billy just lay on her bunk grinning.

The next thing I knew I was in this cell with nothing but a mattress, a cover, and a potty. They told me to take all my clothes off. I absolutely freaked, and they said I had a choice—either to take them off or they'd take them off for me. They gave me a nightie to wear and took my clothes away. They shut the door and I was alone. Then I felt a rush of emotions; contentment, peace, harmony, and the butterfly feeling of excitement you get when something good is just about to happen, like just before going on holiday. That's how I used to feel each time I was put in solitary and the door was shut.

I was told I was really aggressive, kicking and banging the door, swearing at everybody that came near. When the toughest two girls in the prison came to the door, I'd told them to f___ off and that I'd take them out any time they wanted. I don't remember any of that. Then it was morning, and these girls were shouting that they are going to get me. I was absolutely petrified, wondering what the hell they were going to get me for. What had I done? I kept shouting through the door, "I haven't done anything, why do you want to get me?"

I was put before the governor, and she asked me why I'd lit the fire. I couldn't admit that I didn't know that I'd done it, so—and I know this is going to sound daft—but sometimes I used to wait and see what would come out of my mouth. I said something like, "I ain't sorry I did it." She asked if I'd do it again, and I said given half the chance then I would. My punishment was seven days' loss of pay and seven days' loss of privileges. I got put back in the strip cell, and I was absolutely petrified because I knew those girls would kick my head in when I was let out. I got taken out on exercise with two officers, and those girls screamed abuse at me but they couldn't get me. Then I had to go to see the doctor and was asked about the fire. Because I couldn't remember anything, I started to make stuff up and said I was going to burn the cell down if I could get paper and matches. I was all blasé, like I didn't know what I was saying. I was trying to get out of trouble, but I didn't know what I'd done in the first place.

Then I was taken to the hospital wing. My memory is that it was safe and nothing bad happened. It was really good as you were out all day from your cell and there was television and music. There were a couple of women on there in for murder, and they used to look after me and gave me jam sandwiches. My Mum visited, and I had cigarettes and sweets sent in.

When I went to court the following week, I thought I was going to be bailed to a children's home. Suddenly this solicitor stood up and said, "Your Honour, while in prison the prisoner set fire to her cell. She's classed as a security risk at this time. We recommend she's remanded back in prison." The magistrate agreed. I wasn't frightened this time because I knew I was going back to the hospital wing. I was there for two and a half months and was then sentenced at the Old Bailey to Borstal.

I was in Borstal for seven and a half months. It was like being in a locked-up, secure children's home. Most of us were between 15 and 18. We did sport, and I worked in a factory making boxes. I made that fun by mucking around. I know all the stories now, but I don't remember anything bad happening. I had a really good time and didn't want to go home. On my release the plan was for me to go back to London, but a change in probation officer led to me going home, then in Suffolk. My new probation officer, an ex-policeman, was a really nice guy whom I liked, and he really tried to help me.

At home, my Dad was extremely violent a lot of the time to my mother and to me. On Boxing Day I smashed the kitchen up and scared my sister and brother, but I have no memory of doing it. My probation officer told my Mum that I wasn't the only problem. He got my Dad, an alcoholic, into hospital to dry out. I used to go out a lot, made some friends at a youth club, and had a couple of jobs at holiday camps. Mum and Dad moved up north, and after the jobs didn't work out I joined them but hated it. I was nearly 18 and got a job with Community Service Volunteers working in a children's home in Birmingham. I hated that, too, because they lived like a family. I couldn't cope; it was all very alien, and for whatever reason I didn't feel safe at all. I left and went straight to London.

I slept on the streets, or in hostels whenever I could get a bed for the night. I loved the streets. I loved the excitement, and there was always something going on. I used to sleep on Euston Station just where it said "The Queen opened this station." The station always felt safe, like it was a home thing, a good feeling.

Then one day I ended up in University College Hospital. They told me I'd taken an overdose and nearly died. After that they sent me to the Henderson Hospital in Surrey for therapy. I don't know what happened there, except that I had a good mate and I climbed out of the window one day and ran back to London.

In Euston one night a policeman arrested me. I don't remember, but they said I kicked him. I was transferred from the British Transport Police to the Metropolitan Police, and they wanted to search me again. They said I went berserk and it took six or seven coppers to get me handcuffed and into the cell. The next day I was taken to court accompanied by six policemen. The officer in charge said that it was a bit over the top, as she knew me as an affable kind of kid. She'd had a call saying they were transferring a very dangerous prisoner! The magistrate was going to give me a fine, but I told him if he did I'd go out and do it again. He said

I was a danger to myself and remanded me to prison for three weeks for psychiatric reports. The court laughed when I said, "I just want to say, Your Honour, thank you very much. Going back is like going home."

I was sent to the psychiatric wing—known as the muppet wing—and they were drugging me up to the eyeballs. To be honest, I don't remember those three weeks. I remember being petrified on getting a visit from the probation service and being told I'd got to go into a probation hostel. I wanted to stay in prison, but the crime wasn't enough to keep me there.

While in the hostel, from what I gather now, I was heavily drinking and was violent and aggressive. I couldn't understand that, because I didn't drink. By then I thought the world was out to get me. One night, four of us went out: three girls and one guy. We had no money. To me it was just a game, never personal. I was lookout, and they robbed this bloke. The next thing I knew was being told by the girls that the guy had bottled the bloke and taken his money. I thought, "Shit, that's stupid." Then we all went to the pub, spent the money, and went back to the hostel to bed.

I was woken by a knock on my door at 6.30 a.m. to be told that the police were there. They said, "You are under arrest on suspicion of murder." I was absolutely petrified. The other two girls got arrested too, but the guy got away. We were taken to different police stations. I was taken to Kentish Town for questioning. I was screaming and going ape. They gave me cigarettes to calm me down. I kept saying, "I haven't murdered anybody." When I got questioned, I told them straight away that I'd been lookout in the robbery and where and when it happened. I asked if the bloke was dead, and they told me he was still alive but there had been a man bludgeoned to death in the Euston area. I fitted the description, and because of the level of crime I'd committed they were questioning me. All I could think of was Pat. I'd been introduced to her by a friend in Euston. She looked similar to me, and I gave them her name. She ended up in Holloway at the same time as me. I was charged with robbery, taken straight to the magistrates' court, and remanded to Holloway. That was January 1980, and I was 20.

In April, I was sentenced to eighteen months, in Court No 1 at the Old Bailey.

I loved prison. For me it was a safe, caring place. I had good rapport with the prison officers and a good bunch of mates. You got a bed and three square meals, and it provided all I needed. I never understood how I got the reputation I did, like when Pat said, "Me and you are equal." And yet somehow I got to be a trustee on the nursing station. I loved it, but at the same time I smuggled drugs and got paid. It was all a game. I could never understand how I got to spend so much time in solitary confinement. For me it was the safest place, and I read comics and books and listened to all around. The time sped by.

When I was eventually released to a hostel at the age of 22, I was scared. Although all the staff wanted to help, within two weeks I was trying to plan how to go back to prison.

The next thing I knew I was remanded for two weeks for hitting a policewoman in the mouth in the toilets at Euston Station. I have no memory of that at all, but they showed me a photo of her. I was bailed, and when it came to court I was expecting six months, but I was given a suspended sentence and two years' probation. I was given a place in a Salvation Army hostel and was a day patient at a psychiatric clinic.

Rob's story

My name's Rob, I'm 12 and I live in London round Euston most of the time. London's all I've ever known. I'm pretty much a cockney boy, fast on me feet and quick with the wit when it's needed. I get myself out of trouble as much as I can because I'm always in it. When there is any danger, me legs is well fast. All I've ever known is sleeping on the streets. I know how to get away with things, how to get food and drink, what to say to make people feel sorry for you so they give you money and stuff. I'm kind of cheeky, so sometimes I could get myself arrested but I don't because I talk myself out of it. I could see trouble before it happened and I used to leg it. I used to be well mad with myself if I couldn't get away or if I hadn't seen trouble coming.

It's really hard living on the streets, lots of bad stuff happens. People don't really see you as a person, just this thing in the corner of their eye. Sometimes they look at you with pity and other times as if they hated you, like you was an eyesore. People spat at me, kicked me, and called me names, "You're scum you are, scum." My job was just to stand there and grit my teeth when that happened.

You were always hungry and cold, even in summer, like me bones was cold. There was this place on Euston where they'd bring drinks and sandwiches for the people on the streets and I used to get hot chocolate. I love hot chocolate, it warms your belly right up. They were nice and used to talk to you and ask if you'd got blankets or if there was anyone they could ring for you. They knew I was just a kid, but they never told on me. I used to make sure there was no police around.

I liked looking at the peoples' faces and imagining where they lived. Sometimes we'd go up west to the "Dilly" [Piccadilly]. I used to like the lights and the warmth and people with their kids. I don't have a Mum and Dad, never did. All I ever knew was the streets I had to look after myself and be on my toes all the time.

Sometimes the coppers was alright, but sometimes they'd chase you and try to catch you. My legs was fast and I used to well run but sometimes not fast enough and bad things happened, not to me, but to others. My job was to stop it from happening but I couldn't always stop it.

Day was alright because you could hide around people, but at night it was harder. One night the coppers caught us. My mates got away but I didn't. They took me down these stairs at Euston Station, got me arms behind me back. They thought they were well hard; a lot of them and just me. They took me right down these passages to a hosepipe. It was October, it was freezing and they hosed me down head to foot and then walked away laughing. I hated them.

Sometimes we got a bed for the night but not often. I don't remember having a bed, but I think we did.

Damien's story

My name's Damien, I'm 16. I had my first experience of psychiatric stuff when I was 13. I don't remember much about anything else really. I'd find myself stuck in this office talking to this geyser about life and the universe. They used to talk shit. They didn't have a clue about my life and what was going on. I used spin them stories because I knew the git outside would beat the shit out of us when we got home if I said anything out of order. I tried it once, tried to raise the flag so to speak, about what was going on at home but the shrink was crap. He went and got the old man in and told him everything, so I figured don't ever tell a shrink anything again.

Basically I used to tell them lies. After a while you know what they are looking for and you just play the game because they don't want to know the truth. The truth would just blow their mind but hidden in there I left a little message. Not one of them really ever saw it. I guess it was just too well hidden but I figured if they really wanted to understand me, they'd read the message.

Over the years they said we was emotionally disturbed, had a behavioural problems and borderline personality disorder. They treated us with drugs for schizophrenia and psychosis. The drugs they gave you blocked out the pain. I didn't want them but I took them because I knew it helped those that needed help.

They didn't listen to the message. It didn't matter who I talked to. I'd say at some point in every conversation, "Things get really black and I can't keep everything quiet and that's when CHAOS ensues." I'd always talk about blackness and things out of control. They should have asked what was out of control. WHAT PART OF CHAOS DIDN'T THEY UNDERSTAND? I think it's a simple message.

I don't remember much about prison, like a blur really.

Artful Dodger's story

We call me the Artful Dodger, bit of a Jack the Lad but brilliant to have around in a crisis. I don't get caught up in arguments, life's too short for that. For me life's about having a laugh, a bit of fun and when things go tits up and shit then finding the funny side of it. If you don't, you're buggered.

I've been nicked a few times and found myself in police cells. You crack a joke with someone, start bantering and wind up the pigs. That's your job to wind them up.

I made the court laugh when the judge remanded us to prison for psychiatric reports. I said, "I just want to say, Your Honour, thank you very much. Going back is like going home."

I pretty much liked prison. Talk about screw baiting, it was the best time ever. Lock-up time's heavy in the nick and you've always got the squealers and the screamers. It used to do my head in so I'd hide under the beds and things in other people's rooms. They used to have to keep unlocking all the cells until they could find me. It was a joke, just a bit of light humour in the midst of what was a load of shite really.

I used to get on with all the screws, that's my job you see. Some of them were evil gits. Sometimes we'd be locked up for a long time and I'd sing anti-screw songs. It winds them up! In solitary I'd get a bit of a rapport going with the screw on duty, cracking her a few jokes and she'd come and chat to me because she was bored. You've got to remember they're doing life—me, I only had to do 18 months. Without a laugh and a joke we wouldn't be here, so I'm pretty important but if you start asking me deep questions, I'll piss off.

Coppers can be grumpy sods and I think they done bad stuff but if you laugh and crack jokes they haven't got you have they?

You don't always want to be doing the heavy stuff do you? Let's be real, I know what's gone on, I ain't stupid. I looks at it this way, I can't turn back time, I can't make it so we didn't sleep on the streets or go to prison or get beaten up but I can let the bastards know they ain't got to us and can have a laugh. That's the greatest weapon. When they are doing something really bad to you, you just smile and they hate it, trust me they hate it more than anything. Got a powerful tool eh?

But I'm also likeable, extremely likeable. Who else gets a 21st birthday party thrown by the screws? You can't live what you haven't had but you can live and laugh now.

Jay's story

My name's Jay and when I was 12 I was raped by my brother. I didn't like having sex but people thought I did. I hated it. I always found myself in situations I couldn't get out of. I used to let the boys have sex, like I couldn't say no. In my head I'd say no but somehow I knew that sex was what I was supposed to do. Sometimes they were boys and sometimes men. It was horrible what they done. I thought I'd been born to be a slut and a whore and that my role in life was to have sex with men.

And then one day I found myself in prison. The officer had opened the cell door and this girl said, "My name's Billy and I'm a lesbian." I knew I was going to have to have sex with her but I couldn't do it. I got some paper together and set a fire. I went away after that.

Another time, I found myself in a room and this woman came in. Everyone knew she was the psycho of the wing, a really bad woman. I found myself looking at her and I knew what was going to happen and I couldn't do it. I didn't let the women touch me. After that I don't remember much about prison.

One time I found myself in the police cells. That's how my life was really, I'd find myself in situations and wonder how I got there and why it was always me that had it done to them. A policeman wanted to do things to me. He made me take my top and bra off. I did what he asked and he looked, because the cell door was shut. The next day we got let out and I found myself in a café with him. I don't know how I got there. He was asking me what happened in prison and what girls did to other girls. I didn't want to talk about it because I think it's disgusting. And then I knew what he was going to do. He took me up the side of the café and had sex with me. I knew there was no point in telling anyone because who was going to believe that a policeman raped me. He said that I'd done it because I wanted to but that wasn't true. I just found myself in that position.

Now I know it wasn't my fault.

Billy's story

My name is Billy, I'm 16 and I've been raped. I couldn't stop it. I was in prison on the hospital wing. This woman comes at me, I tried to stop her. She shouldn't have done it, I was a bloke . . . you can't rape a bloke. I don't understand how it happened and the screws didn't stop it, nobody stopped it. They knew she got out of her cell and they figured something had happened to me. It was easier to close the cell door and pretend it hadn't happened and then no one got into trouble. I saw her every day after that and she goaded me about what she'd done to me.

I hate women because they pretend they're your friend and then they rape you. I should have stopped it but I couldn't, she was strong.

They said she had "paranoid schizophrenia", was a sociopath and had psychopathic tendencies. The things she said she was going to do to me . . . it was easier to let her do what she had to do. Hard for me to live with the consequences but better that than we die. She raped my mind as well as my body. She could have killed me and I knew that no one was going to help me, so I took it so tomorrow we'd wake up and be alive.

I love life now though. I'm the computer wizard and I can do loads of things. I make things work. I couldn't make things work then but I've got a purpose now.

Molly's story

My name's Molly, I'm 12, and I'm thick. I got to be thick. There had to be one person and I got chosed. I'm alright about being thick.

I'd just be sat in the police station all the time. I'd be minding my own business and I'd feel this yank on my neck and I'd be looking at a policeman. I like policemen. They give you apple pie and ham sandwiches and they like you.

They asked funny questions. "When you were drinking, who were you drinking with?" I'd tell them the truth that I'm not drinking with no one cos I'm not. Then they'd ask me if I'd seen things and I'd tell them I didn't. Sometimes they'd get cross and say, "Are you thick or what!" And I'd say, "Yes, I'm thick."

I was always in trouble. I've never not been in trouble.

I done prison too. I only ever saw the governor. She always asked me about things I'd done. And you had to call her Ma'am. I'd say, "Yes Ma'am, I didn't see nothing." She'd say, "But you hit a prison officer." I'd say, "But I can't have done, I can't have done, I didn't see her." Then she'd get cross and I'd tell the truth. I'd look her right in the eye and say, "I didn't see her, I didn't do it honest. I wouldn't hit a Prison Officer. Why would I want to hit a Prison Officer?"

Another time, she wanted to know why I'd lit a fire. This is silly because I didn't light a fire but I had to say, "Because I wanted to keep warm and if I want to keep warm again I'm going to light another fire." I just knew in me head that's what I'd got to say. So she said, "So you're going to light another fire?" I said, "Well I'll have to if I want to keep warm."

Samuel's story

My name is Samuel and I'm 16. I was called Sam in prison.

One woman called Pat had bludgeoned someone to death. Jay was scared there would be another rape and so I came along. Louise had a naivety about her that drew the gay girls. I had a job to do. I had a deadly look. I looked Pat in the eye, and she said, "You and me are equals." After that she said I was her buddy. I got a name there.

One time in the dormitory a girl was goading us and goading us. I knocked her back teeth clean out of her mouth, and then I disappeared before anyone would figure out it was me. No one was going to touch Louise.

I hated it in solitary. It was there I felt all the hopelessness and despair.

HJ's story

I'm HJ and I'm 14. I've always been around and I stopped at 14 because I didn't trust adults. What happened when we were little is another story.

It's complicated. My Mum and Dad were authority figures in their job and were friends with social workers and doctors. I had a pure hate of authority, and my agenda was to get them before they got us. I was so angry.

I did the crimes. I wanted to hurt that woman in the park because she looked at me like I was scum, like I was dirt on the floor so I gave her a slapping I wanted her to remember. That's how it works.

It was me that shouted at the judge, "If you send me to a f_____ children's home I'll run away."

The first time we got to Holloway they did a strip search and the screws were shouting and I lost it. I was shouting and swearing and chucking things about. As I was leaving reception I heard, "Watch that one, she's trouble."

In solitary for the first time, two tough gay girls came to the door shouting abusive stuff about the things they were going to do. I lost the plot. I was so angry, kicking and banging and yelling at them to f____ off. I hated it there. Time used to drag and you'd hear voices all around you. The pain of the world was wrapped up in that place. You never knew whose eye would be at the spyhole—a friendly, hard, or gay screw. I hated the isolation and the sparse room.

Prison was a living hell where there was rape and violence and drugs were rampant. Prison never went to sleep. There was the noise, people screaming, doors banging, always somebody hassling you, even in solitary.

On the streets, I did the out-of-control things and the police were always sending for reinforcements. After Rob got hosed down by the police I went berserk, absolutely f_____ berserk.

I punched the policewoman in the mouth. I wanted her to hurt. She was coming for Louise and Louise hadn't done anything wrong.

On the streets everything was out of control and I needed to make it safe. For me prison was about containment. If you get into a fight on the streets you can be knifed and killed within seconds. I liked fighting. I wanted to hurt people that were getting at us and I was so angry. But in prison you can have a fight and the agro-bell goes.

You see, I really thought I was capable of killing someone. When we were arrested on suspicion of murder I knew I hadn't done it but I could have done. So, I kept us safe by going to prison because I was afraid of what I might do.

But it was more complicated than that. I never knew why we had to go inside. It's going to sound nuts, but I just knew we weren't safe but I never knew why. I've always known I've got to make it safe. Prison wasn't safe in one sense, but I knew whatever was trying to get us couldn't get us behind bars. It was the only time I didn't feel that sense of foreboding. We knew they couldn't get us in prison but I don't know who couldn't get us.

We all covered up for Louise and some of us worked together, me, Sam, Jay, and Billy. It was H who got us to be a trustee on the wing so we could walk round on our own.

We were not the normal bag: an affable, funny teenager and then with the next breath we could have pinned you to the wall. We became hard, we fought, we were cocky, vulnerable, easygoing, funny, affable, dangerous, known to be bordering on evil, very bright, very thick, whatever we needed to be, and there is one thing we agreed on—we had to stay alive.

The jigsaw

I [S.C.] met Louise at a therapy weekend, when she was about 40. Some time later she asked to see me privately, to continue the work she had experienced there.

Since her release from prison, some twenty years earlier, she had not re-offended. She was released to a Salvation Army Hostel, from where, with much support, kindness, and containment, she had started to build a new life. She soon moved to a flat, gained O and A Levels, then a degree in Youth and Community Studies, and eventually a job as a youth worker.

Louise had no idea she had dissociative identity disorder, but she was familiar with the concept of having an inner child and also an inner adolescent she called "H". She felt quite stable in 2002, when a job opportunity arose abroad, working in a residential home for adolescent girls. While working there, she made discoveries about the running of the home that led to its closure, and also to her own breakdown: "It was like, in a dark place full of cobwebs in my head, about ten doors were blown open at the same time." She returned to England unable to work or cope with life emotionally and physically. All medical investigations showed nothing.

I started to see her again, and gradually different parts—as she prefers to call them—made themselves known. A diagnosis of DID was made at the Pottergate Centre for Dissociation and Trauma in March 2004.

Working with Louise—and with the different parts that are continuing to appear—is like putting together pieces of a jigsaw that is becoming increasingly complex and multidimensional. The emerging picture tells a story of how and why she developed DID. Neither Louise nor any one of her parts knew the whole story, except Silent Witness, who couldn't speak.

From what I now understand, dissociation began as a baby in order to survive sexual and physical abuse by her father. Jay explains, "We're all built on that: a needy, abused baby who never knew when she was going to get hurt." He was violent and abusive towards her mother and her siblings, and yet to the outside world he was a caring family man.

H explains: "Each of us was created when it got too much. It was like passing the baton in a relay race, and we did it all the time. It made it possible to look ok, and no one knew what was happening. Without realizing it, in Louise's head were different boxes or rooms. When Louise's Mum came home, Louise wouldn't remember that she'd been beaten senseless and thrown in a cupboard. That happened to Mary and she was in another room." When parts such as Jay, 12, who was created to take sexual abuse from men and boys, couldn't cope, they created other parts. When faced with lesbian abuse and violence in prison, Jay created two more boy parts, Billy and Sam.

An interesting point about this system is that after HJ was created, very early on, both she and Louise went on creating her own parts. Subsequently, the internal system is made of two "subsystems", who are aware of their "genealogy".

But far from making the picture gradually clearer, time made it more complex and multidimensional. Louise began to experience flashbacks, and memories began to emerge of a different level of abuse. It appears that Louise's father was involved with paedophile rings, and she was being taken to "paedophile parties" by the age of 3 years, for which he was paid. Another group of parts emerged that was created to deal with this layer of abuse.

As Louise and I were working on this chapter, she experienced more flashbacks, and new parts emerging. They belong to yet an-other layer in the system and have begun to make sense of why prison was seen as a "safe place". "We knew they couldn't get us in prison, but I didn't know who couldn't get us", said HJ.

A group of thirty 7-year old children were created to cope with what appears to involve ritual abuse, probably satanist. H explains: "This world was built on fear that you can't begin to comprehend as an adult. I knew this existed but I don't know the details. I'm the only one who knew, apart from Silent Witness."

These new personalities are revealing other types of horrific abuse. Some of them are too traumatized by what they have wit-nessed and experienced to be able to speak. As H has put it, "It was a world that even scared her father."

Working with Louise and her personalities has brought many complex challenges. Dealing with my own vicarious traumatiza-tion, through bearing witness to her accounts, is one challenge. Another is working with offender-parts. My first encounter with Sam, for example, was a look that sent a cold shiver down my spine. Louise was very frightened of aggression, in view of her history. Could therapy trigger criminal behaviour? What about my safety, if they saw me as a threat? How could I work safely with them?

There were also ethical questions: at first, HJ and others did not want any therapy! Then Rob showed me around Euston Station, where he slept and where he was hosed down. Others told me their stories at Kings Cross. HJ took me to Kentish Town Police Station, where Louise was taken when arrested on suspicion of murder, and finally to Holloway Prison. None of these "excur-sions" fitted with my training.

The role of crime in Louise's life is enormous. Strikingly, the crimes for which she had been imprisoned are the least significant. Underneath that layer of "ordinary crime" are the far worse events that she had lived through from babyhood, and which her DID enabled her not to know about. She is now facing that reality.

CHAPTER SIX

Dissociative identity disorder and criminal responsibility

James Farmer, Warwick Middleton, & John Devereux

The seemingly bizarre symptoms of dissociative identity disorder (formerly known as multiple personality disorder [MPD]) have long fascinated and polarized psychiatrists, psychologists, philosophers, and lawyers. Constructions offered in the courts range from that of one person with a fundamentally disintegrated psychic structure and prone to flashbacks and hallucinations in multiple sensory modalities, through to that of a person with a number of personalities or person-like states of consciousness inhabiting the same body (Saks, 2001). Philosophers ponder such questions as whether a DID sufferer possesses a continuing sense of personal identity and consciousness and can perform actions as a true agent (Sinnott-Armstrong & Behnke, 2001). Lawyers and judges, who rely on expert witnesses (particularly psychiatrists) to give evidence in courts on DID, face particular challenges in cases dealing with the criminal responsibility of DID sufferers. As a result, the judgments show contradiction and inconsistency in their reasoning, further adding to the confusion faced in future cases [*State of Washington v Wheaton* (1993)].

This chapter explores the inconsistencies in psychiatry and law, both as to the definition of DID and how a diagnosis of DID may be used by a defendant in the criminal justice system. The first part of the chapter explores the psychiatric literature on the meaning and content of DID. In the second part, an exploration is made of relevant common-law cases on DID. The final part of the chapter suggests a way forward in the DID debate.

The psychiatric view of DID

The diagnostic criteria for DID are set out in the *DSM–IV–TR* (APA, 2000). It is defined essentially by two dissociative phenomena: amnesia [criterion (c)] and the presence of alter personalities or dissociative identity states [criteria (a) and (b)]. In the accompanying text in *DSM–IV–TR*, three further phenomena are mentioned—flashbacks, voices, and conversion symptoms.

Dell's (2002, 2006) exhaustive review of published series concerning DID, however, describes 21 dissociation-related symptoms: (1) memory problems; (2) depersonalization; (3) derealization; (4) trance; (5) flashbacks; (6) child voices; (7) persecutory voices; (8) voices commenting on one's own actions; (9) voices arguing or conversing; passive-influence experience such as the Schneiderian first-rank symptoms of (10) "made" feelings, (11) "made" thoughts, (12) "made" actions, (13) influences playing on the body, (14) thought insertion, and (15) thought withdrawal; (16) somatoform/conversion symptoms; (17) identity confusion; (18) disconcerting experiences of self-alteration; (19) time loss; (20) fugues; and (21) finding evidence of one's behaviour for which one has no memory.

The symptoms of depersonalization, derealization, trance, identity confusion, "made" feelings, "made" thoughts, "made" impulses, influences playing on the body, thought insertion, and thought withdrawal are not mentioned at all in the *DSM–IV–TR* description of DID. The remaining eleven symptoms are either directly specified by, or can be inferred from, the five clinical phenomena that *DSM–IV–TR* relates to DID, although "voices giving instruction" are only one type of hallucinatory voices (Dell, 2002, 2006).

Putnam (1997) modified and amended the scheme first devised by Lowenstein (1991) to arrange the great diversity of symptoms found in DID patients into clusters of symptoms. He divides them into primary dissociative symptoms and frequently associated post-traumatic symptoms, secondary symptoms, and tertiary symptoms. All the symptoms of DID identified in the literature by Dell (2002, 2006), along with post-traumatic symptoms of DID, are described by Putnam as being primary pathological dissociative symptoms or associated post-traumatic symptoms. These symptoms contribute to the high co-morbidity that DID shares with other trauma-spectrum disorders such as post-traumatic stress disorder (PTSD), borderline personality disorder, somatization disorder, and drug and alcohol dependency (Middleton & Butler, 1998).

Dissociation is defined in *DSM–IV–TR* as "a disruption in the usually integrated functions of consciousness, memory, identity or perception of the environment" (APA, 2000, p. 477).

Fink (1988) expresses the purpose of dissociation succinctly:

> The *I* . . . is not maintained in dissociation, and dissociated content becomes *not me* experience. The essence of the pathological process operative in MPD is designed to satisfy one injunction: That did not happen to me, it happened to another. [p. 43]

Daniel Stern (1985) postulates that, in an infant, the development of a sense of core self is the first temporally, and this lays the foundation for subsequent developmental stages.

He defines the core self as:

> the physical self that is experienced as a coherent, wilful, physical entity with a unique, affective life and history that belong to it . . . [and which] generally operates outside of awareness. . . . [p. 26]

According to Stern, a number of self-experiences, which are "self-invariant", are available to the infant, even in the early period of life.

> (1) *self-agency* . . . authorship of one's own actions . . .: having volition, having control over self-generated action . . . and expecting consequences of one's actions . . .;

(2) *self-coherence*, having a sense of your being a non-fragment-ed, physical whole with boundaries and a locus of integrated action;

(3) *self-affectivity*, experiencing patterned inner qualities of feel-ing . . . which belong with other experiences of self; and

(4) *self-history*, having the sense . . . of a continuity with one's own past. . . . [p. 71]

It is plausible, then, to expect that pathological dissociative symp-tomatology would reflect malfunctions of these factors in a DID sufferer. As examples, Stern suggests that an absence of agency can be seen in catatonia, hysterical paralysis, and derealization and in some states when authorship of action may be taken over (p. 71). Fink (1988) agrees with Stern's last example. Putnam and Trickett (1993) also observe that volition may be disrupted by passive-influence experiences, often accompanied by intense de-personalization, when individuals seem to act against their will or their better moral judgement.

Memory can also be disrupted. This is well illustrated by gaps in autobiographical memory, which are often in the form of trau-matic memories (van der Hart, Bolt, & van der Kolk, 2005). The person, therefore, may lack access to experiences and/or a set of values or societal norms that enable him/her to choose construc-tive ways of resolving challenges.

Pathological dissociation also causes a disruption to conscious-ness. Dissociative identity states are *states of consciousness*. A change to a different state of consciousness can occur in other disorders, but DID is unique because changes in states of consciousness are between dissociative identity states (Putnam, 1997).

DID and the criminal justice system

Having examined the symptomatology of DID and briefly in-vestigated how it disrupts memory, identity, consciousness, and perception of the environment, we have a foundation to discuss the criminal responsibility of DID sufferers. However, by limiting our investigation to "criminal responsibility", we bring into play a number of assumptions and presuppositions that underlie the criminal justice system.

Schopp (2001) comprehensively examines these factors in liberal democracies and sets out a number of foundational propositions:

> An agent is one who acts, exerts power, or produces an effect. Accountable agents exert power or produce effects in a manner that qualifies as accountable under some normative criteria. Legally accountable agents are accountable according to the criteria specified by some legal institution that embodies underlying principles of political morality that govern that society. Principles of criminal responsibility in the United States and other liberal democracies include criteria that reflect the conception of accountable agency required to justify their holding a defendant answerable to the criminal justice system. [p. 318]

> [Competent practical reasoners] can understand that certain conduct violates the prohibitions of the system and anticipate that such conduct will elicit aversive consequences in the form of criminal punishment . . . [and] can make use of this knowledge in the process of practical reasoning through which they direct their behaviour. [p. 320]

> This process of practical reasoning requires an awareness of self as an identity that extends over time. An individual acts in a manner calculated to attain future rewards or to avoid aversive consequences in the future precisely because that person experiences himself as an extended identity who maintains a relatively stable set of preferences and priorities over time. [p. 320]

Schopp's point here is that only "competent practical reasoners" qualify as legally accountable agents in a liberal democratic society's criminal justice system and can be held criminally responsible for their actions. By "competent practical reasoners", he means people who have access to a relatively stable set of "wants, beliefs, interests and principles that provide that person's extended sense of self" (p. 328). They use those attributes to choose how to act or react in situations that confront them in everyday life, in order to conform their behaviour to the requirements of the criminal law.

We suggest that DID patients may also fall into the category of persons who are *not* "competent practical reasoners". Gaps in autobiographical memory (including lessons learned from past experiences and the significance of "cause-and-effect" relationships), mean that DID patients have, at best, erratic and disjointed access to "a relatively stable set of wants, beliefs, interests and principles that provide that person's extended sense of self" (Schopp, 2001), as do people who suffer from psychotic illnesses such as schizophrenia. We suggest, however, that DID sufferers frequently face multiple deficits in respect to developed self-hood (boundaries, affect stability, and life-narrative: Middleton, 2005). Schopp's definition of "a competent, practical reasoner" presupposes that the individual possesses an extended sense of self. DID sufferers lack an integrated sense of self because they suffer from disruptions to the invariants that constitute the sense of core self, as outlined by Stern (1985), and changes in consciousness to other dissociative identity states that encapsulate, and are organized around, "a prevailing affect, sense of self (including body image), with a limited repertoire of behaviours and a set of state-dependent memories" (Putnam, 1989). A fragmented, unintegrated sense of self is not an extended sense of self. By Schopp's definition, a DID sufferer may fail to meet the criterion of a legally accountable agent and not be criminally responsible.

It is our contention that the current rules governing unsoundness of mind do not adequately cover the case of a DID sufferer. The *M'Naughten Rules* [*R v M'Naughten* (1843)] and their variants are based on an implied jurisprudential paradigm of "one person, one body" or, in psychiatric/dissociative terms, "one integrated psychic unit, one body". The *Rules* ask questions that are more appropriate for a sufferer of schizophrenia or another delusional disorder where he or she would be found of unsound mind if deprived of the cognitive capacity, the moral capacity, or, in some jurisdictions, the volitional capacity. Although DID sufferers are generally able to understand what they are doing, to engage in goal-directed activities, and to know right from wrong, they lack a unified sense of core self and are disrupted across the indicators of memory, consciousness, and perception of the environment by pathological dissociative symptomatology. Other mental illnesses exhibit some of these characteristics, but they are not all present together, nor with the intensity or pervasiveness seen in DID.

Court decisions from various common-law jurisdictions add to the conceptual difficulties raised by the application of the *M'Naughten Rules* and do little to clarify the issues raised or provide consistency of approach. The decisions emanate from courts in state and federal jurisdictions in the United States, with three exceptions, and disclose three approaches in determining the criminal responsibility of DID sufferers.

The first approach focuses on the mental state of the *dissociative identity state that is present or in executive control at the time of the offence.* In *State of Ohio v Grimsley* (1982), the appellant Grimsley appealed a conviction of driving under the influence of alcohol. She suffered from MPD and claimed that because her primary personality, "Robin", was neither conscious of nor had control over the actions of her secondary personality, "Jennifer", at the time of driving, she should be exonerated. Secondly, she claimed that her primary personality "was not conscious of the wrongfulness of the secondary personality's acts and did not have the ability to cause that personality to refrain from driving while drunk" (p. 1076). The court focused, correctly, on the appellant's state of mind at the time of committing the offence. However, it went on, in rejecting the appeal, to explain that the evidence failed to show "that Jennifer was either unconscious or acting involuntarily" (p. 1075). The court continued: "There was only one person driving the car and only one person accused of drunken driving. It is immaterial whether she was in one state of consciousness or another, so long as in the personality then controlling her behaviour, she was conscious and her actions were a product of her own volition" (pp. 1075–1076).

In *Kirkland v State of Georgia* (1983), the defendant was charged with two bank robberies. She entered banks when they were almost empty, wearing a similar disguise, and was armed with a pistol. She pleaded not guilty by reason of insanity on the basis that she suffered from psychogenic fugue, a mental condition that the court found was very similar to MPD. She claimed that the robberies were committed by "Bad Sharon". The trial court concluded that the fugal personality was "a well-developed, rational and conscious personality, so for legal purposes, we will not distinguish them" (p. 564). The court reasoned that "[t]he law adjudges criminal responsibility according to a person's state of mind at the time of the act; we will not begin to parcel criminal accountability out among the various inhabitants of the mind". She was found guilty but mentally ill. The Georgia Court of Appeals followed *Ohio v Grimsley*, saying that the personality did so with knowledge that it was wrong and with criminal intent.

In *Kirby v State of Georgia* (1991), the defendant was charged with fraud to the sum of nearly $300,000. Evidence was given by a psychiatrist that a bad personality, "Kirby", had committed the offences while a good personality, "Bill", had been suppressed. He was found guilty but mentally ill. On appeal, he argued that *Kirkland v Georgia* should be over-ruled because of advances in the study of MPD. The appeal court dismissed the appeal but ruled that, while MPD was better understood, the appellant had not shown that a person suffering from MPD should be excused from criminal responsibility. The court ruled that "in the case at bar, it is undisputed that appellant was conscious and acting under his own volition. Moreover, appellant was able to recognize right from wrong and was not suffering from delusional compulsions" (p. 335).

In *R v Hamblyn* (1996, New Zealand), the accused was charged with using cheques with intent to defraud. She was diagnosed by two psychiatrists to be suffering from DID. The psychiatrist called by the defence gave evidence that "alter" personalities controlled the behaviour of the accused at the time of the offences but knew right from wrong, even though the host personality did not know of, nor control, the actions of the alters. The Crown psychiatrist's opinion was that, at the time of the offending, the host was in an alternate state of consciousness but was still the host and was therefore responsible for her behaviour. The court found that "the alters were not insane, so at the time the offences were committed, the body was being directed by a sane mind" (p. 229). The court followed the reasoning in *Ohio v Grimsley, Kirkland v Georgia*, and *State of Hawaii v Rodriguez* (1984) to conclude that the appellate courts had endorsed the "specific alter" approach of examining the sanity of the alter committing the offence. The Court of Appeal found no error of reasoning or finding of fact, noting that the court's finding was in accordance with the opinion of the Crown psychiatrist and based on the approach of the appellate decisions mentioned above.

The second approach involves examining the mental status of the *host personality at the time of committing the offence*. This approach was used in the case of *United States v Denny-Shaffer* (1993). The trial judge directed the jury in accordance with the first approach, saying that the alter(s) should be focused upon, as to whether those alters satisfied the insanity defence. The accused appealed because the experts agreed that one alter personality, "Rina", perhaps with another, "Bridget", controlled the actions of the accused at the time of the kidnapping. However, the experts were unable to agree whether the defendant's dominant or host personality consciously participated in preparing for or carrying out the offence. Furthermore, a defence expert was unable to decide whether the alters acting at the time of the abduction knew that this was wrong. The trial judge rejected the accused's defence of insanity, for lack of evidence. The Appeal Court ruled that the trial judge was "unreasonable in restricting the focus of the court and jury to the alter or alters cognizant of the offence, and ignoring proof that the dominant or host personality was not aware of the wrongful conduct" (p. 1014) and that "the trial judge erred in rejecting evidence respecting the ability or inability of the host or dominant personality to appreciate the nature and quality or wrongfulness of her acts in kidnapping the infant here" (p. 1021).

The third approach makes pivotal *the state of mind of all alter personalities at the time of the commission of the offence*. In *Hawaii v Rodriguez* the court appeared to follow the first approach, saying, following *Ohio v Grimsley*, that "it was immaterial whether the defendant was in one state of consciousness or another, so long as in the personality then controlling the behaviour, the defendant was conscious and his or her actions were a product of his or her own volition" (p. 618). However, the court then went on to say, that "since each personality may or may not be criminally responsible for its acts, each one must be examined under the American Law Institute-Model Penal Code competency test" (p. 618).

We suggest that there are a number of problems in these approaches. In respect of the first approach, while the appellant was claiming unsoundness of mind at the relevant time, the court appears to analyse criminal responsibility in terms of consciousness and voluntariness, a quite different basis of exculpation. Second, and more importantly, the courts attribute the possibility of conscious, purposeful, and voluntary activity to dissociative identity states. In other words, the court attributes the status of a person to the secondary personality and, by necessary implication, is subscribing to the notion that an individual can be more than one person. Third, the focus becomes the criminal responsibility of the dissociative identity state that was in executive control at the time, instead of the criminal responsibility of the *person as a whole*. Does what is "right or wrong" for these psychic entities hold for the person as a whole? Can such entities be regarded as "competent, practical reasoners" and, therefore, as legally accountable agents? We contend that the answer to both questions is in the negative. Furthermore, changing the focus to the host or dominant personality does not resolve this difficulty. The host personality is another dissociative identity state—its "dominance", if there is any, is by virtue of its being the one that interacts with the world more often in a period of time. Fourth, all approaches focus on only one symptom (dissociative identity states) from the plethora of symptoms documented in the literature and may produce a skewed understanding of DID and its effect on criminal responsibility.

The dilemmas facing the courts and the resulting inconsistencies are well illustrated in the line of cases involving William Bergen Greene, heard before the Supreme Court of Washington. Greene, a ward of the state at age 8 years, endured ongoing physical and sexual abuse including a gang rape at the age of 12 by three older boys. Convicted of car theft in 1972, Greene spent most of his life in prison following convictions for burglary and repeated sexual offences. He participated in a sex-offender treatment programme, in which he was diagnosed with major depression and DID. Released in 1992, he voluntarily continued outpatient therapy, found gainful employment, and maintained a non-abusive, intimate relationship and a number of healthy friendships. In 1994 Greene's condition deteriorated in the context of a fire at his employer's facility, resulting in him being scheduled to be laid off. His therapist, concerned about his suicide risk, instructed him to telephone her daily. Alarmed by the content of a conversation, she called at his home to evaluate the need for hospitalization. While she was in his apartment, Mr Greene committed the offences of taking indecent liberties and first-degree kidnapping (Frankel & Roseman, 1999).

At his trial, Greene claimed that one of his diagnosed alternate personalities, "Tyrone", who manifested as a 7-year-old, was the prime instigator of the offences and was incapable of knowing right from wrong. He also asserted that at least four other personalities exchanged executive control of his body during the attack. He wanted to present evidence of his mental illness and his behaviour during the incident from an expert psychiatric witness and from his therapist, the complainant. The trial judge, however, in a pre-trial application by the prosecution, excluded testimony from the proposed expert witness, ruling that such evidence did not meet the requirements for admissibility in *Frye v United States* (1923) and that it failed the test for relevance under Rule 702 of the *Washington Rules of Evidence*.[1] He also excluded the proposed evidence concerning Greene's state of mind, either by Greene himself or by the complainant. The defendant was convicted and sentenced to life imprisonment.

On appeal (*State of Washington v Greene*, 1998), the Court of Appeal reversed the verdict and held that DID is a generally accepted mental diagnosis in the mental health community and was relevant to the defences of insanity and diminished capacity. The court remanded the case for a new trial. The prosecution appealed.

The Supreme Court of Washington, in *State of Washington v Greene* (1999), agreed with the Court of Appeal that DID was generally accepted within the scientific community as a diagnosable psychiatric condition and that expert evidence concerning DID met the *Frye v United States* standard for admissibility. However, the court went on to say that the trial court was correct in refusing to admit expert testimony concerning the defendant's dissociation because "[s]cientific principles that are generally accepted but are nevertheless incapable of forensic application under the facts of a particular case are not helpful to the trier of fact because such evidence fails to reasonably relate the defendant's alleged mental condition to the asserted inability to appreciate the nature of his or her actions or to form the required specific intent to commit the charged crime" (p. 74). The question, said the court, was "whether and how the symptoms of DID are relevant to the legal concepts of insanity and diminished capacity" (p. 74).

The court then examined *State of Washington v Wheaton* (1993). In that case, the defendant was charged with second-degree robbery after she took money from an open cash register, threatened an employee, and took the employee's driver's licence. She was diagnosed as suffering from MPD, and expert evidence was given that, at the time of the offence, an alter personality, "Cassie", was in control of the defendant's body and that the host personality, "Dea", was not conscious, nor in executive control, nor had independent knowledge of the offence. The expert witness also said that he had elicited "Cassie" and concluded that she was sane according to the *M'Naughten Rules*. This expert said that he was "unable to render further opinions regarding the remainder of the defendant's personality system, particularly the host personality, because there is simply no scientifically acceptable way to assess the mental state of alter personalities who were not co-conscious at the time of the crime" (p. 350). A second expert gave an opinion that the correct focus was the global approach, which would result in a finding of insanity whenever the host personality was not in executive control or co-conscious at the time of the offence. The court, however, dismissed the opinion of that expert, saying,

> Insofar as Dr Lindsay's testimony may be construed as defining two possible legal standards for assessing the sanity of a criminal defendant suffering from MPD, that testimony encroaches on the responsibility and authority of the courts to decide such legal matters. As the court has recognized, criminal responsibility is a legal, rather than a medical or scientific problem, and, in a larger sense, it is a social question. Insofar as Dr Lindsay's testimony relates to the disorder and how it affects individuals suffering from it, and how it may be related to a determination of sanity or insanity under the *M'Naughten* standard, it may be accepted as the kind of medical/scientific testimony which can assist a court in deciding the legal issue. [pp. 353–354]

The court in *Washington v Greene* (1999) then went on to examine cases from other State appellate courts—namely *Hawaii v Rodriguez*, *Ohio v Grimsley*, and *Kirkland v Georgia*—and concluded that these cases were insufficient to convince it to hold that the "specific alter" approach or any other approach was the appropriate standard by which to judge criminal responsibility. The court observed that their decision in *Washington v Wheaton* was based

> on the lack of consensus, both in the courts and the medical community, on the proper forensic method to be used. We find ourselves in no better position today than we did then. . . . Our decision stemmed directly from the fact the scientific community had not yet developed an accepted method to assess the sanity of a criminal defendant diagnosed as suffering from MPD. [pp. 74–75]

A defence expert, Dr Olsen, was prepared to testify as to the sanity of the alter in control at the time, but he was not prepared to testify as to the sanity of Mr Greene, saying he was "not sure who Mr Greene is", although he was able to say that if he was the host personality, he appeared sane, but if he was the alter personality, he appeared insane. The court acknowledged the force of Dr Olsen's comment, saying,

> Dr Olsen's comment . . . reflects the fundamental nature and difficulty of the question with which we are presented. That is, when a person suffering from DID is charged with a crime, the question becomes, 'who is the proper defendant?' A determination of sanity in this context can be considered only subsequent to the determination of who (which alter personality) should be held responsible for the crime—the host, or possibly one or more of the alters. This, in turn, related to the scientific possibility of identifying the controlling and/or knowledgeable alters at the time of the crime. [p 78]

Scheflin (2003) commented that the court misunderstood the expert's proposed testimony. "What the expert was really, and accurately, saying was that he could not address the purely *legal* question of whether the defendant should be judged based on the alter's state of mind, the host's state of mind, or the persona as a whole. This is not a scientific issue" (p. 3).

The nature of the court's dilemma in this case is shown in a further passage from the judgement.

> We recognize that ultimately the question of who should be responsible for the commission of a crime is a legal one. In the present context, however, the answer depends largely on

the ability of the scientific community to assist the courts in understanding how DID affects individuals suffering from it and how this may be related to a determination of legal culpability. We do not exclude the possibility that there may be a case in which the sanity of a defendant suffering from DID can be reliably evaluated. However, based upon the evidence and testimony presented here we do not find this is such a case. Accordingly, we must agree with the trial court that the proposed expert testimony in this case was inadmissible under ER 702 because it would not have been helpful to the trier of fact. [p. 78]

Greene then applied to the United States District Court for the Western District of Washington, seeking a writ of habeas corpus. The petition was granted. The prosecution appealed to the Federal Court of Appeals. In *Greene v Lambert* (2002), the court held that the exclusion of all evidence of DID violated the defendant's right to present a defence, contrary to the Sixth Amendment of the United States Constitution and affirmed (by majority) the grant of the writ.

Greene was re-tried on the same charges in 2003. Greene presented expert testimony of two experts, Drs LeReau and Steinberg. They testified that Greene did suffer from DID and was not malingering. The complainant testified about her observations concerning Greene's behaviour during the attack and gave her opinion that an alter personality was in control of his actions during the assault. Greene did not testify. The State contested the diagnosis and called three experts who testified that Greene did not suffer from DID. The court directed the jury to consider Greene's insanity defence in accordance with the *M'Naughten Rules*. (The State had sought directions that the jury should assess Greene's state of mind using either a "specific alter" approach or a "unified approach"—that is, to assess Greene's mental capacity as a whole and ignore the boundaries between alters. The defence had submitted that the jury should use either the "specific alter" approach or the "host approach".) Greene contended that the trial court violated his Sixth Amendment rights to present a defence and his right to a fair trial by refusing to adopt a legal standard for assessing DID and failing to direct the jury on how to evaluate insanity based on DID. In *State of Washington v Greene* (2006), the Court of Appeals of Washington re-iterated its conclusions in *Washington v Wheaton* (1993) and *Washington v Greene* (1999), saying that the "adoption of a legal standard must be 'soundly based' on a record that clearly supports one of the competing approaches for assessing insanity based on DID" (p. 7). After examining the record, the court concluded that the evidence did not support any of the competing approaches and that the trial court's refusal to adopt a DID-specific legal standard was not an error (p. 8).

We may summarize the conundrum in which courts find themselves. Experts are looking to the courts for a legal standard or pronouncement as to how, when they give evidence, to assist the courts concerning the criminal responsibility of DID sufferers. Courts are saying that experts should not give opinions as to what legal standard should be adopted, as this is the province of the courts, or give an opinion as to criminal responsibility. However, they ask the scientific community for guidance as to what that standard should be, but they then say that the scientific community is unable to give that guidance because the evidence from the experts, in a particular case, does not support one of the competing approaches, or there is insufficient consensus in the scientific community as to how to judge the sanity of a DID sufferer. Therefore, in a particular case, the trial court may rule that the evidence does not provide a sound basis for the adoption of a legal standard or is inadmissible because it is unhelpful to the trier of fact. Additionally, if the matter comes before an appeal court, and the trial court chose a standard by which to judge the defendant's criminal responsibility or rejected the proposed expert evidence as being irrelevant or unhelpful, the appeal court may say that the trial court was entitled, in the exercise of its discretion, to find that the defendant was of sound mind. A further difficulty, as Appelbaum and Gutheil (2007) point out, is that little attention has been devoted to translating these competing standards into clinically meaningful terms: "Law and psychiatry have yet to find a common basis for discourse" (p. 231).

Although there seem to be problems with using the *M'Naughten Rules* to judge DID cases, there is one instance in which the modified *Rules* may be helpful. Some jurisdictions have added a volitional capacity. This is sometimes referred to as the "irresistible impulse" test and asks the question whether the defendant is deprived of the capacity to control his or her actions. This point arose in *Orndorff v Commonwealth of Virginia* (2004). The defendant was convicted of second-degree murder after shooting her husband in the course of a domestic dispute. The defence retained two psychiatrists to give opinions as to whether she had any psychiatric disorders relevant to her committing the offence. Both doctors testified that she was suffering from a dissociative episode precipitated by the trauma of her husband's death. The jury found her guilty. However, before the sentencing process began, the defendant was observed to be behaving strangely at the prison, saying that she was 12 years old, had done nothing wrong, and should not be in an adult prison. She was examined again by one of the defence psychiatrists, who gave an opinion that the possibility that the defendant was suffering from DID had to be excluded. She was transferred to a state mental health facility because of doubts that she was competent to stand trial. After eight months, she was judged competent to stand trial.

During this detention, she filed a motion requesting a new trial due to after-discovered evidence, the equivalent of fresh evidence. The fresh evidence, she contended, was a firm diagnosis of DID, testified to by two further defence experts, Drs Dell and Lowenstein. Both of the original defence experts concurred with the new diagnosis, and all agreed that she was not malingering. Dr Lowenstein's opinion was that the defendant

> suffered from an impulse that was sudden, spontaneous and unpremeditated. At the time of the crime, Ms. Orndorff was overwhelmed by symptoms of DID and personality disorder NOS, and possibly, by acute and/or chronic posttraumatic stress disorder and depression NOS as well. Accordingly, she was so impaired by these diseases of the mind that she was totally deprived of the mental power to control or restrain her acting to harm Goering Orndorff. [p. 393]

That motion was denied, and she was sentenced to 32 years' imprisonment. The defendant appealed the denial of the motion for a new trial. The Court of Appeals, by majority, allowed the appeal, saying "that she had done everything that was reasonably possible prior to trial to discover grounds for a plea of not guilty by reason of insanity . . ." (p. 397). A new trial was ordered.

A defence of unsoundness of mind based on the volitional

capacity was also raised in *Re: Wigginton* (1990, Queensland). The defendant and three other women were charged with the murder of a man they had picked up and taken to a park. Wigginton stabbed him on a number of occasions. Police investigating the death found a keycard belonging to the defendant pushed into the toe of one of the victim's shoes. On examination by a defence psychiatrist, while under hypnosis, the defendant was found to have at least five identity states, one of whom, "Bobby", confessed to the killing. She was diagnosed with MPD. On a reference to the Mental Health Tribunal, the tribunal ruled that there was significant disagreement between expert witnesses as to the validity of the diagnosis and whether the defendant was suffering from MPD. The tribunal doubted that the defendant was suffering from a mental disease or a natural mental infirmity and "that, even if at the time of the alleged offence, the patient was in a state of mental disease or natural mental infirmity, it did not deprive her of [any of the three capacities]" (p. 32). The *Queensland Criminal Code*, s.27, includes a capacity to control one's actions.[2] The tribunal also rejected a defence of diminished responsibility based on MPD being an abnormality of mind.[3]

In *Re: Gleeson* (2007, Queensland), the defendant was charged with 72 counts of fraud committed over a year. The defence expert testified that she suffered from DID which qualifies as a disease of the mind and that she was deprived of the volitional capacity because she could not control switches to the offending identity state, "Stephanie". The expert who reported for the court testified that she suffered from borderline personality disorder and dependent personality disorder, which were not diseases of the mind, and that she was not deprived of the volitional capacity. The court declined to determine whether DID was recognized within the scientific community as a diagnosable psychiatric disorder. Accepting the opinion of the court-appointed expert, it did rule, however, on the basis of the evidence presented, that it was not persuaded that the defendant suffered from a disease of the mind and that she was not deprived of any capacity, including the volitional capacity.[4]

A defence based on the volitional capacity seems, however, to have little applicability as it is available in only a limited number of jurisdictions in the common-law world.

DID—a way forward?

We propose that the focus of attention should be modified in the cases of DID sufferers and suggest some tentative propositions and proposals.

> Only persons can be judged as criminally responsible or not. The focus should not be on any or all of the dissociative identity states but on the mental state of the person as a whole.

> The DID sufferer should be viewed fundamentally as a person with a fragmented, non-integrated sense of core self.

> The mere existence of DID does not entitle a person to a defence of unsoundness of mind.

> Particular attention should be paid to the symptoms of, or associated with, DID found in the literature and present at the time of the offence, and their effect on the behaviour of the individual.

> The extent of the dividedness and fragmentation of the person in terms of his or her sense of core self, as shown by the resulting dissociative symptomatology, and the seriousness of the impairment to his or her ability to function as a "competent, practical reasoner", should be the core components of any standard by which the criminal responsibility of DID sufferers is judged.

> The court should specify the issues that it wants expert witnesses to address in order to assist it in determining the extent and effect of the two suggested core components. These should include, but not be limited to, the following:

  • Results from psychological tests to determine whether the defendant suffers from, and exhibits symptoms of, DID. Controlled testing should be used to examine the existence of amnesic barriers—whether uni- or multidirectional—between identity states, access by identity states to autobiographical and traumatic memories, and the extent, if any, of co-consciousness.

  • Whether the defendant has been subjected to physical, sexual, and/or emotional abuse. Details should be supported by corroborating data such as medical records, Department of

Child Welfare (or their equivalent) records, statements from witnesses such as other siblings, and police statements.

- Evidence from independent sources who have observed, prior to the offence, symptoms of DID and differences in behaviour, particularly changes in appearance, demeanour, dress, vocabulary and speech, evidence of memory dysfunction (such as failure to recognize that person or a person well known to the defendant), plus observations of responses to auditory hallucinations.
- Reports from previous psychologists and/or psychiatrists and records of any hospital admissions, including any previous diagnoses.
- Interviews with the defendant, not utilizing hypnosis, without any therapeutic component, avoiding leading questions, and, where possible, recorded by audio-visual means. Interviews should focus on the unaided eliciting of dissociative identity states, relationships between identity states, the "power structure" existing within the psychic system, whether identity states sabotage the activities of other states or cause trouble for each other, switching between identity states, sharing of information between states, triggers precipitating switches, and whether, and to what extent, switches can be controlled.
- Investigations as to whether the offence was committed in a flashback state, during a re-enactment of past trauma, or as a result of a perceived threat of abuse.
- Documentation and explanation of evidence of the intensity of delusions of separateness, such as suicide attempts and instances of self-harm.
- If possible, recordings of conversations with the identity state that committed the offence, the motive(s) for doing so, perception of the environment at the time of the offence, and the involvement and/or knowledge of other identity states and their ability to control the active identity state.

We hope that our analysis, and our propositions and proposals for a modification of the rules governing unsoundness of mind for DID sufferers, will stimulate debate in this unsettled area of the criminal law.

List of cases

Frye v United States (1923) 293 F. 1013 (D.C. Circ.)

Greene v Lambert (2002) 288 F. 3d 1081 (United States Court of Appeals for the Ninth Circuit)

Kirby v State of Georgia (1991) 410 S E 2d 333 (Georgia Court of Appeal)

Kirkland v State of Georgia (1983) 304 S E 2d 561 (Georgia Court of Appeal)

Orndorff v Commonwealth of Virginia (2004) 44 Va. App. 368 (Court of Appeals of Virginia)

R v Hamblyn (1996) DCR 217 (District Court, New Zealand); C A 99/97 (unreported, judgement delivered 1/7/1997); Court of Appeal, New Zealand

R v M'Naughten (1843) 10 Cl. & F. 200; 8 E.R. 718

Re: Gleeson (2007) Supreme Court of Queensland sitting as the Mental Health Court—Philippides J (Proceeding No. 0232 of 2006, judgement delivered 1st October, 2007)

Re: Wigginton (1990) Supreme Court of Queensland sitting as the Mental Health Tribunal—Ryan J (Judgment delivered 21/11/1990)

State of Hawaii v Rodriguez (1984) 679 P 2d. 615 (Hawaii Court of Appeals); certeriorari denied, 469 U.S. 1078 (1984)

State of Ohio v Grimsley (1982) 444 N E 2d 1071 (Ohio Court of Appeal)

State of Washington v Greene (1998) 92 Wn. App. 80 (Washington Court of Appeals)

State of Washington v Greene (1999) 139 Wn. 2d 64 (Supreme Court of Washington)

State of Washington v Greene (2006) Wash. App. LEXIS 2498 (Court of Appeals of Washington, Division One)

State of Washington v Wheaton (1993) 850 P 2d 507 (Supreme Court of Washington)

United States v Denny-Shaffer (1993) 2 F. 3d 999 (United States Court of Appeals for the Tenth Circuit)

Notes

1. *Washington Rule of Evidence*, 702 (ER 702), states: "If scientific, technical or other specialized knowledge will assist the trier of fact to understand the evidence or to determine a fact in issue, a witness qualified as an expert by knowledge, skill, experience, training or education, may testify thereto in the form of an opinion or otherwise."

2. *Queensland Criminal Code*, s.27(1), reads: "A person is not criminally responsible for an act or omission if, at the time of doing the act or making the omission, the person is in such a state of mental disease or natural mental infirmity as to deprive the person of capacity to understand what the person is doing, or of capacity to control the person's actions, or of capacity to know that the person ought not to do the act or make the omission."

3. Determination of the question of unsoundness of mind and fitness for trial in Queensland may be made by a Mental Health Court, pursuant to the *Mental Health Act 2000* where a single justice of the Supreme Court of Queensland sits, assisted by two psychiatrists. The court sits as a Commission of Inquiry. At the time of the reference of *Re: Wigginton*, the Supreme Court sat as the Mental Health Tribunal, pursuant to the *Mental Health Act 1974* and exercised substantially the same powers as now. The defendant may still choose to have the questions of unsoundness of mind and fitness for trial determined by a jury during the trial, or after, or instead of, a reference to the court.

4. The first author appeared as counsel for the defendant, and the second author gave expert evidence for the defence.

CHAPTER SEVEN

When murder moves inside

Valerie Sinason

T he police were in a quandary. On the one hand, the woman's detailed descriptions had correctly pinpointed where
the body had been found and the marks that would be
found on it. A 28-year-old graduate, part-time language teacher
and part-time housewife, Mrs Carly Lawrence (not her real name),
was sharp and articulate. The details had not been in the press,
and there was no way she could have guessed it without prior
knowledge. On the other hand, some details were completely
wrong. Her descriptions of clothes and weather did not tally in
any way with what was known. She could not describe the alleged
murderers. Also, her concepts of time and place and how long it
took to get from one particular house in a built-up city to the rural
scene of the crime were woefully inadequate. The police are, on
the whole, not geared up to psychological complexities. Time and
place are pivotal pieces of information for police but often the least
relevant, or the least held in mind, for the witness or the victim.

Carly had also shocked the police by providing information
about a further murder she had allegedly been involved with.
The person she named was, it was found, someone who was
missing—although, tragically, someone who was not missed. The

teenager she named was known to services and police as someone who was in and out of trouble with a history of allegations
of abuse in care homes that were never proven. Carly provided
graphic details of how she was forced to commit the murder
and how it was accomplished. The sturdy police officer warned
her of the dangers of making such statements. Even with a body
not found, it was possible to be convicted for murder. Laws on
duress did not exist to cover such acts. As is common with such
allegations, the witness is treated either as a vulnerable victim
incapable of adequate testimony or as a possible perpetrator due
for sentencing.

And so it was that the police came to consider Carly as a vulnerable witness and link her to their vulnerable-victim coordinator.
Regrettably, they did not feel they could make use of her statements at present. The police, in common with other professions,
are still struggling to adequately support vulnerable witnesses,
although enormous strides have been made. Instead of seeing
psychological health issues being a natural response to trauma,
police, like other professional workers, can see it as an automatic
sign of witness unreliability. And, of course, Carly Lawrence was
certainly unreliable.

She would make an appointment to speak with the vulnerable-victim coordinator and then cancel it at the last moment. She
would ring urgently to say she had a new crucial piece of information and then disappear for several days. On her return she would
appear different, brusque, and withholding. She would deny any
previous contact between herself and the officer. However, the
vulnerable-victim coordinator was a profoundly empathic woman
who had a deep sense of the authenticity of Carly's experiences.
In the end her evidence was not used in court, although the police
had no doubt she had genuine links to the murder. And Carly was
left alone for the terrible repercussions that followed.

For Carly, of course, was not just Carly. She also contained
Charlie, Carlotta, Crasher, and Candida. And her "C" team were
different ages and genders. They also all had different views about
aiding the police in their enquiries, different fears and hopes, different allegiances and attachments. Carlotta rang the "family"
immediately after Carly had spoken to the police. She was ten
years older than Carly and was programmed to know the steps

needed to avoid maximum punishment. They would not escape it totally—neither she, nor Charlie (who was 17 and obedient to the family out of terror), nor Crasher (of indeterminate age and made to be a torturer), nor the little child, Candida. Only Carly would escape it. But of course she would always recognize the signs of punishment on her body. And if Carly's treachery was deemed to be beyond even a severe punishment, then all of them might die, even Crasher.

There was no victim-protection programme that would extend to cover their needs. Fine had she been reporting a terrorist attack or even a major supplier of heroin. But a DID witness referring to gross criminal offences that occur in rituals, including murder, does not get such a chance. Had that been available, Carlotta and Charlie could have dared to change sides, could have dared to step out from the dark terrorized loyalties of their upbringing, could have supported Carly instead of leaving her alone and would have brought Crasher with them, despite the savagery of his response, and little Candida could have been brought to safety.

In fact, it would have been the other way round. Candida, like many of the youngest little ones in a DID system, was outspoken in her longing for "cuddles that don't poke" and her wish to get away from the nasty frightening people with their masks and whips and cruelties. Indeed, although she was only aware of it at times, some of Carly's courage came from seeing Candida's sketches of tortured children. "I want to stop this going on. I can't let her suffer that again", she would cry.

Carly's partner George could not protect her. He had been chosen for his ability to close his eyes to signs of trauma. They had always had separate bedrooms, and Carly had never told him about the dangers to her on ritual nights. Nevertheless, his love and companionship were crucial for her, much as she feared admitting any attachment. "If I admit how much he matters to me, they might hurt me by threatening to kill him." Like almost everyone we have met who has gone through cult abuse, she had been brought up to see that anything loved could be destroyed and used against you.

And therapy, even with a team structure, left huge gaps. Not that the gaps were huge compared to what therapy and counselling clients usually received from the NHS. Carly had a primary therapist who worked with her once-weekly with a double session, a subsidiary therapist who worked once-weekly with her with a single session, a neighbour who popped in twice weekly, and a partner who loved her. If need be, she could call Samaritans in the middle of the night, in the times when none of her regular team were awake. And she could phone the vulnerable-victim coordinator, who cared about her and had slowly and painfully learned to understand her situation. However, even that package, big by other standards, let the dark frightening clouds of trauma in.

After disclosing to the police, Carly was even more beset by traumatic memories and thoughts. Her body was covered with bruises, and she knew she had also been raped. She was aware of losing time more frequently and of coming to with a racing heart and enormous sense of terror. She did not want to go to her GP or to a sympathetic forensic place like The Haven. She could report the murder she was sure she had committed, and she could report the murder by unknown masked people. But DNA tests might reveal something she could not bear to know. After a few weeks, a terrible certainty entered her mind. She was going to be killed by the cult because she had broken the cardinal rule—she had spoken out. And she had spoken out about a murder too.

On her desk Crasher left notes in envelopes with words like "DIE" or "YOUR TURN" in places where George would not find them—not that he ever looked. Even though Carly was aware she could never have managed a man with his eyes open to her plight, she regularly felt a sense of heaviness and despair that she should have chosen such a literally sleeping partner.

After a particularly terrible night, she woke in pain and found the word "Die" carved in her flesh. Her therapist and team reminded her that killing her would prove to the police that everything she had said was true. Also, as Carly had specifically requested, the team would not withhold anything from the police in the event of her death. They also made clear they had never heard of the threat being carried out, even though, to keep obedience in the ranks, the abusers often took their victims to the edge of no return. However, such words were useless coming from those who had never had to suffer such extremes. The important issue was that Carly was sure she was going to die and that whether she locked her doors and windows and lay with a phone in her hand, it would all be useless.

The particular day came. Carly did not understand why that date had a particular emotional and charged meaning for her, but she knew somewhere that it was a harbinger of terror. Her team arranged to call her in shifts except, of course, no one was free between 11.30 p.m. and 7 a.m. "You never do the graveyard shift", she laughed wryly. Carly was also aware that she, unusually, was hugging Dana, the soft little puppy that belonged, she knew, to Candida. Usually she threw it away contemptuously or hid it. But this last week she had drawn comfort from it.

And of course it was on the graveyard shift that something happened—but not to Carly.

> Candida knew it was going to be bad. She was lying huddled and naked in the Black Cave. Candida did not see that she was living in a nice terraced house with a small back garden that belonged to Carly, whom she loved. On nights like this, the house and garden felt like a cartoon from another television channel. The Black Cave, however, she knew was real. She had been put in it for lots of sleeps when she was tiny and it was cold and open to the elements. Sometimes big people she did not know hurt her there, hurt her very badly. But then she was bad so she knew they had to do these things to her. Sometimes it was people whom she knew. George felt a long way away. He was a nice big man who never hurt her. And her therapist was a long way away too. Carly was gone. Waiting for them to come, she could not even think of cuddles that did not poke, or of Dana her soft little toy puppy. All she could think of was how bad she was and how she should die so nobody could ever see how bad she was.

> And that was the moment she saw Crasher, coming towards her with the knife raised.

When Carly woke up in the morning she was aware of enormous bodily pain followed by a sense of loss. She looked around her bedroom. Everything was in place. The sun poured through the light curtains, and everything shone. The photographs on her dressing-table, the folded clothes ready for the day, nothing was out of place. Except in her. Every part of her hurt, and she dreaded going to the toilet. But worse than the thought of any injuries was the sense of loss.

"I think Candida has been killed", she said to her therapist. Suddenly, a wave of feeling connected her to little Candida. Tears poured down her face. Carlotta and Charlie had to come out to help her. Carlotta was pragmatic about it. "That's what happens when you tell. Lucky it wasn't Carly." Charlie was terrified. Crasher did not appear.

Carly found that this internal murder hurt her far more than the external one she had successfully reported and been validated over. She went around her house picking up any communications from little Candida—drawings, scraps of paper, dressing-up clothes. She scanned her photograph albums looking for Candida. Terrible nightmares showed her Crasher rushing towards her holding a ceremonial knife. She found it harder to go to sleep, frightened of what dreams she might dream. But more than all of this, she was terrified of how she was haunting herself and haunted by herself. "I have got a murderer inside me. Don't give me the therapy crap about how everyone can feel murderous. This is different. Crasher is a murderer. He has murdered a child and I want him arrested and he is inside me. I am going to tell the police."

In a virtual-reality world like Second Life, such a thing might be possible. But in the real multiple layers of life within a multiple system, there was no police officer who could arrest an internal personality for an internal murder, however sympathetic the vulnerable-victim coordinator was.

Just as the outside police failed to take Carly's evidence further for the external murder, so was there an impasse with the internal murder. Carly grew more and more fearful until a particular event happened two weeks later.

Feeling less bruised, and able to walk, she happened to visit a large bookshop. On one shelf was a title that caught her eye, *Delta of Venus* by Anaïs Nin. She did not buy it, but the word *delta* caused a frisson that excited her. Later that day she watched a film about the Nile Delta and realized more consciously that the word *delta* had a strange meaning for her.

Her therapist commented that as Carly was a linguist, did she have any other thoughts about the word *delta*? Carly immediately commented that it was Greek and, although she had never learned Greek, she knew enough to start reciting, "Alpha, beta, gamma, delta", with increasing intensity and a certainty that these words had terrible meaning, at which point there was a slight switch and Crasher came out for the first time.

"Don't get her into that," he snarled. "I am warning you. You wouldn't like to see what happens if you get into that." The therapist said hello to him and how pleased she was to see him and added that she knew perfectly well what a delta was and it was probably him. Crasher's snarl disappeared, and he looked genuinely shocked. "How do you know what a delta is? It is secret." The therapist told him it was all over the internet, and the programming never worked properly anyway.

Delta is one of many "programs" that are used by some groups in order to control people's minds. It is an "assassin program", which is claimed to be a military mind-control program. However, despite the attempts to create slave robot Manchurian Candidates, human attachment proves to be a much stronger and more robust entity. Crasher was slowly freed from his delta programming. Carlotta was able to rethink the program that made her call the family each day, and Carly was slowly restored. Little Candida remains dead, in an unknown internal graveyard. She was loved and is mourned no differently than had she been an "outside" death.

The vulnerable-victim coordinator stays in touch with Carly, while the external corpse—the real external-life corpse—has been buried in a named grave, and no arrest has been made for the murder.

Integration versus internal murder

In my introduction to *Attachment, Trauma and Multiplicity* (Sinason, 2002), I wrote the following: "At one level the idea that five different people could all have timeshares in one body seems absurd. And yet, it is both delusional and real and all at the same time". I added the point that understanding this paradox takes us into a new way of conceptualizing the human mind. However, it was too late. I had already caused hurt to the very people whose existence I was writing about through my inability at that point to really take on board the unique existential predicament of every human, whether internal or external, a singleton or a multiple. I made a promise to the protective or supportive alter who brought this to my attention, Alex, that I would remove the word "delusional" from my description of him in the next edition.

Candida was a small child whose whole existence was a matter of degrees of pain. She existed in real time in a shared external reality as well as an internal reality. Those who loved her, including her therapy team, displayed the same bereavement behaviours as they would towards a child who was not part of a timeshare. Crasher, Carlotta, Carly, and all the others were all people with a conscious and unconscious, with mixed motivations, with different upbringings and experiences of the world, and with different responses to pain, to joy, to relationships.

While some people with different levels of dissociation might be able to become co-conscious or choose to integrate—or "multigrate", as Southgate (2002) calls it—not everyone can or wants to. Integration implies a seamless continuity of memory that allows a "delusion" of seamless continuous identity. In other words, an "integrated" person can behave like a 2-year-old one moment, a teenager the next, and return to his or her chronological age the next moment, with a continuous memory uniting those emotional changes.

For those who do want to integrate—which means they sense that their mind has the capacity to undertake such a task—the whole issue is how to merge without there being a murder. The moment someone is seen as "only an alter", or, worse, only a "delusion", then we are on a dangerous road in showing, even where we do not at first realize we are doing that, a denigration of the value of human life.

CHAPTER EIGHT

When the imaginary becomes the real: reflections of a bemused psychoanalyst

Phil Mollon

S ome years ago, I had been working in psychotherapy with a woman artist, Natasha, for a couple of years or so. Her paintings displayed vivid abstract images of violent intrusions, explosions of red engulfed by a menacing black. From the beginning, she had presented narratives of sexual and other forms of abuse by her father, a senior manager in public services. He had, according to her account, behaved during her childhood—and even now that she was adult—in extremely controlling ways, telling her repeatedly that everything in the house, including her, belonged to him and that therefore he could do as he chose with his "property". She appeared to have a confused perception of her father, perceiving him at one moment as a monstrous perpetrator of crimes against her, and at other times believing that he was the only one who loved her. These conflict-laden perspectives were also at times expressed in the transference. For example, she once tearfully exclaimed that I obviously did not care about her because I did not abuse her.

"Natasha" is not an actual person but a composite representation, a narrative device based on impressions of a number of cases.

There were other puzzling features of Natasha's presentation. For example, her style of communication would often be elliptical, as if endlessly circling around some horror or forbidden information, hinting but never stating clearly what she meant. If I were to ask her to clarify what she might be referring to, she would appear suddenly very anxious and would then seemingly shift to another subject. At other times, she would talk with great clarity and coherence.

Sometimes, Natasha would appear very childlike—for example, on one occasion crouching on the floor in the corner of my office, saying nothing but appearing terrified. Subsequently, she claimed to remember nothing of this session. On another occasion she left a message on my answering machine in a frightened childlike voice asking for my help because people were hurting her. Again she appeared to have no subsequent recollection of leaving this message.

I had trained in psychotherapy at the Tavistock Clinic and was well versed in conventional approaches to interpreting transference, projection, discerning oedipal and other infantile phantasies, and so forth. Indeed, I believed I was reasonably good at this. However, I found patients such as Natasha deeply troubling. The strange dissociative episodes, followed by apparent amnesia, were completely unfamiliar to me. I knew about "splitting"—a defensive manoeuvre of keeping good and bad mental representations apart, emphasized in the work of Melanie Klein (1946), Kernberg (1975), and Grotstein (1981)—but these substantial divisions within Natasha's psyche seemed of a different order. Moreover, while I was at home with phantasy—the play of conscious and unconscious imagination, the language of dreams, and the various ways in which the forbidden desires of the psyche are given disguised expression—the continual actual intrusion of the forbidden in Natasha's childhood and adult years seemed to violate not only Natasha's own life and psyche, but also the analytic process itself. The blurring of phantasy and reality seemed at times to threaten a descent into psychotic confusion for both of us. Natasha apparently believed that her father would follow her, would spy on her at her place of work, and that he had caused her to lose her job on more than one occasion. I had no means of knowing whether Natasha was speaking of an accurate perception or a delusion.

How could we know? She reported her father's abuse to the police on at least two occasions. According to her, the senior police officer she first spoke to became aggressive and hostile on learning the identity of her father and of his affiliation with a well-known secret society. On the second occasion of her attempted reporting to the police, the officer appeared very concerned and said he would follow up her allegations and contact her, but apparently he never contacted her and did not return her calls. One of the clinical dilemmas, in this and similar cases, is the problem of having insufficient evidence on which to determine whether the patient is telling us of a delusion or a conspiracy.

This dilemma became intensified when Natasha began seemingly to recall further dimensions of crimes from her childhood that went far beyond her allegations of her father's sexual abuse of her. She spoke of strange ritual activities, with occult connotations, involving groups wearing robes and other costumes. My consternation and confusion came to a head when she appeared to recall in some vivid detail a ritual murder taking place in a wood sometime during her early years. I had never heard of anything of this kind. No patient had told me of a murder before. Nor, at that time, had there been, as far as I was aware, any reports in newspapers of murders associated with the activities of paedophilic or occult groups. Natasha reported her recollections to a police officer linked to Scotland Yard. She also scoured old newspapers for any reports that could have any bearing on her memory of a murder. However, although there were subtle details that gave her memory an impression of authenticity, she could not recall sufficient context to provide a location or other details that could provide the basis of a proper investigation.

Now the "psychoanalytic" therapy had subtly shifted its focus, from a concern with discerning unconscious phantasy, infantile conflicts, projective processes, and so on, to a preoccupation with something profoundly shocking and forbidden that may have taken place *in the real*. We were no longer dealing with the play of phantasy and imagination, carefully confined within the strict boundaries of the psychoanalytic frame, but with what *appeared* to have been a very serious crime. On the other hand, we did not know—I did not know—whether what I was hearing was an account of a crime or a delusion. To say that this caused me anxiety and confusion would be a profound understatement. Moreover, I noticed that if I tried to speak to colleagues about this, they would react with a mixture of puzzlement, emotional detachment, and an apparent inability to think. I spent many of my own psychoanalytic sessions talking of these matters. It is to my analyst's enormous credit that he did manage to remain thoughtfully receptive to my communications about Natasha and did not immediately assume that she was deluded and that I was pathologically credulous to be considering there might be literal truth in her accounts.

If we suppose for a moment that abuse had indeed taken place in Natasha's childhood, that her father had continued to seek to interfere with her life as an adult, and that a murder had taken place, what were the implications for the psychoanalytic therapeutic process? The therapeutic frame had been violated as well as Natasha's body and mind. We were forced to become preoccupied with disturbing phenomena that rested uneasily between the imaginary and the real. Were they delusional or hallucinatory images, schizophrenic productions—metaphoric symbols of a psychologically murderous childhood environment, perhaps—or were they essentially veridical recollections of real events? With such uncertainty pervading the process, on what basis could I interpret unconscious content? And if I were a cognitive therapist, how would I determine the errors and distortions in her thinking?

At times Natasha would communicate in a highly confused and confusing, albeit intensely affect-laden, manner. She would be angry—with me, her parents, God, her employers, her work colleagues, and the world in general. Any attempt to engage her in a calm consideration of her reports of childhood events would often lead only to highly disorganized and scrambled communications. At other times, she would speak of the alleged events with startling clarity and persuasive detail. She had informed the police, but this seemed not to have led to any further investigation. Her attempts at locating relevant newspaper reports had come to nothing. Medical records potentially relating to early abuse were found not to be available.

I noticed that my role had shifted from the normal psychoanalytic one of listening and interpreting the phantasies and conflicts of the patient's psyche. Instead, I had become preoccupied with questions of the reality and nature of alleged crimes. My psychic stance had been hijacked by that of detective. Moreover, it seemed important to Natasha that I believe her account of a murder, while at other times she would talk as if she had never told me any such thing.

Several hypotheses occurred to me: (1) Natasha was schizo-phrenic and generating delusional and hallucinatory narratives. (2) Natasha had suffered abuse and trauma in childhood, and this had led to a trauma-based psychosis, causing her to generate narratives that were a mixture of truth and delusion. (3) Natasha was suffering from some kind of neurological disorder, or perhaps "sleep paralysis", such that she experienced a kind of "dreaming while awake". (4) Natasha was suffering from some kind of per-sonality disorder, perhaps histrionic or paranoid, that was leading her to generate exaggerated accounts of adverse circumstances in her childhood. (5) A murder had indeed taken place. Throughout the time I worked with Natasha, and since, I did not feel I had sufficient evidence to arrive at any firm conclusion in relation to any one of these possibilities.

How do we know if a person is deluded? This is a rather basic question that is usually overlooked in discussions of psychosis. In order to conclude that a person's belief or account of alleged events is delusional, we would have to know either that the narra-tive contradicts certain obvious realities (e.g. a person's belief that he has died), thus containing a logical impossibility, or that it is in conflict with other facts that we might be able to ascertain. Some-times the seeming bizarre nature of the patient's belief is taken as an indication of its delusional nature. The problem with this kind of criterion is that it relies on the assessor's subjective impression of what is plausible. For example, one interviewer might consider that an account of alien abduction, or of visitation by "men in black" following an observation of a UFO, is so inherently implau-sible that *ipso facto* it must be delusional; others might consider that such an account is unusual but conceivably possible and in line with many similar reports. The content of what is described seems a poor guide as to its veridical or delusional nature. We are on somewhat safer ground if we listen to a patient's account of his or her evidence for a delusional *belief* (as opposed to a narra-tive of events) and we are able to see that his or her processes of reasoning are flawed, that he or she is drawing a false conclusion from essentially ordinary events (e.g. reading special personal meanings into a television news report). Even so, the reasoning processes of many people would not stand up to close scrutiny of logic, and so this criterion too seems somewhat flimsy. If we are simply presented with a narrative of an event, we may have no basis on which to know whether it relates closely to something real that took place out there in the shared world, or whether it is a personal but objectively false perception (Mollon, 2002a).

I have seen many patients in my 30 years of full-time clinical practice in the British NHS. Sometimes I have wondered whether there are people who have a schizophrenic kind of temperament, who do not present with a clear schizophrenic illness, yet are prone to hallucinatory experiences and delusional memories that are not easily revealed to be such. Occasionally I might get glimpses of such phenomena. For example, a patient may claim to recollect that in a previous session I made a certain remark that would seem to me quite unlike anything I might conceivably ever say, or that a particular event took place in the context of the therapy, and I am quite certain that this was not the case. These purported recollections might appear, in general terms, moderately plausible to others—that is, they would not seem inherently bizarre. The patient would appear convinced that these events (e.g. speech acts on my part) had taken place, while I would feel convinced that they had not. On other occasions, a patient might appear certain that a certain event had not occurred, while I would feel in no doubt that it *had* occurred. An example of the latter was when a patient apologized to me for missing her previous session, saying that she had felt too upset to enter the hospital building and so had simply sat in her car for the duration of the session; my belief was that she had indeed come to her session, but had appeared in a very strange state of mind and had spent most of it crouched under a chair.

Two conclusions occur to me. First, the grounds for distinguishing a delusion from a belief or perception that is considered non-delusional are often extremely fuzzy. Second, we may often not be in a position to know whether a client's account of events is essentially true or whether it is the product of some disturbance in the processing or recall of sensory experience. In respect to both these, our position is unlike that of a police officer, whose job it is precisely to ascertain the evidence and determine the objective truth. It may be said that to a large extent, as psychotherapists, we deal with subjective meaning and that figuring out objectively what happened is not our forte. However, this realm of the subjective, our transitional space of psychoanalytic play, may become hopelessly violated when questions of crime enter the picture. The traditional sphere of psychoanalytic investigation is more or less limited to that of the play of conscious and unconscious desire and phantasy, expressive of conflictual psychodynamics. As soon as the notion of an actual crime enters the scene, then this protected realm of the private and subjective is invaded and distorted. Crimes must be investigated and made public; phantasies, on the other hand, are to be interpreted and maintained within the subjective. The separation of these is crucial. The paradigmatic example is that of incest. *Phantasies* of incest are considered by most psychoanalysts to be more or less ubiquitous in children and in the child parts of the mind. However, if this phantasy has at some point become a reality, then we are dealing with a crime, which, in principle, should be investigated by a third party.

Revelations of crimes-that-do-not-exist, appearing in the consulting room, are akin to hallucinations. Both are expressions of the "real" that has been foreclosed in the formation of the symbolic. We might consider the broad realm of mainstream cultural and media discourse as consisting of the dominant symbolic structure determining what we normally believe to be true, possible, and within the nature of reality. Certain phenomena, such as ritual abuse of children within perverse religious groups, do not find a place within this mainstream discourse, other than in the negative ("it does not exist"). The possibility of their reality has no place in this dominant symbolic realm. Thus, when we hear of reports of such things, which are not in the form of negation, the experience is like a shocking hallucination. We do not know what to do with the information. It does not fit, and cannot be assimilated into, the dominant symbolic discourse.

Vanier (2000) defines the "real" in Lacanian terms as follows: "The *real*, which is not the same as reality, is an effect of the symbolic, what the symbolic expels as it establishes itself" (p. 2). The problem we are faced with is the question of whether the image and narrative of "a murder" is a manifestation of a "return of the real", which had been disavowed and foreclosed from the unconscious of the patient or from the unconscious of society in the formation of its dominant symbolic. Often we might not be in a position to know whether either of these two hypotheses is correct.

What can be done to help patients such as Natasha? I will state straight away that I do not believe psychoanalytic work is possible in such cases where the boundary between phantasy and reality has been, or appears to have been, breached to such an extent. The transitional space of play, which forms the analysable psychoanalytic transference, has been breached and thus cannot exist. Efforts to work in an essentially psychoanalytic way with the violated body–mind system are, in my view, likely to lead only to anxiety, confusion, and frustration (Mollon, 2002b). Certainly the work might be psychoanalytically *informed*—and anyone who has undergone the relevant training, and the personal transformation of his or her own lengthy analysis, *becomes* a psychoanalyst and has the particular emotional intelligence and attunement to the unconscious that ensues from this—but the classic focus on interpreting derivatives of unconscious infantile (oedipal) desires and conflicts is much less relevant in the case of the violated mind (Mollon, 1996) than in the case of "neurotic" psychic structures. I feel it is important to acknowledge the limitations of psychotherapy. A little bit of help can be provided in relation to facilitating communication, thought, and collaboration between different parts of a dissociative personality system, strategies of affect regulation can be taught, and a general ambience of support and respect can be offered. Beyond this, our potential for discernment and healing at the boundary of the imaginary, the symbolic, and the real may be inherently constrained.

CHAPTER NINE

Some clinical implications of believing or not believing the patient

Graeme Galton

"**D**o you think I'm making all this up?" asks David, a man in his forties with dissociative identity disorder who has just described to me a shocking and nauseating experience of sadistic sexual abuse that he experienced as a child.

It is my experience that people with DID are likely to describe having experienced severe and ongoing emotional, physical, and sexual abuse from an early age, and it will be extremely important to them that we believe their account. They may also describe committing such abuse themselves. It is possible that these accounts will not be presented until several years of psychotherapy have established sufficient trust that the therapist will take them seriously. The memories of these experiences may be divided between different personalities, with amnesic barriers keeping certain memories from the awareness of other personalities. This means that a memory of an experience may be held by a particular personality and may not be available to a patient's other personalities, leaving those personalities with no knowledge of the experience, or several personalities may remember an experience but the main personality may know nothing of the event. One of the difficulties that can face us as psychotherapists when a patient describes traumatic experiences of emotional, physical, and sexual abuse is the challenge of believing the reality of what the patient is saying, especially if the memories have not been held continuously in the patient's conscious memory. This chapter explores some of the clinical implications of a psychotherapist either believing or not believing a DID patient's memories of extreme abuse and the effect that the therapist's response may have on the patient.

A brief word on the reliability of memory

The issue of whether victims' memories of sexual or ritual abuse are likely to be distorted has been debated with considerable passion and conviction, both within the mental health professions and by others. Many therapists working in this field have come to the view that individuals who have been traumatized are more vulnerable to having both true and distorted memories coinciding (Mollon, 2002a; Ross, 2004; Sandler & Fonagy, 1997; Sinason, 1998, 2002).

The reliability of memories has been especially questioned when the memories have not been held in continuous awareness. In 1995 the British Psychological Society Working Party on Memory concluded that both repressed memory of sexual abuse and false memory of sexual abuse were real occurrences (British Psychological Society, 1995). In 1996 a similar working party established by the Royal College of Psychiatrists had divided views on the subject. The report produced by the working party was criticized by some sections of the college and was not published. Several members of that working party later published a paper on the subject in the British Journal of Psychiatry in which they conclude that "when memories are 'recovered' after long periods of amnesia ... there is a high probability that the memories are false ..." (Brandon, Boakes, Glaser, & Green, 1998, p. 296). This was subsequently disputed in the same journal by van der Hart and Nijenhuis (1998, p. 538), who write, "there is no empirical basis to argue that delayed memories should be met with unusual reservations".

The meaning of truth is exceedingly complex, and as psychotherapists we are primarily concerned with a patient's psychic reality, rather than with what we might call the historical truth that would be required in a court of law. However, the notion of psychic reality does not mean that we can ignore the external reality of our patients' experiences. As psychotherapists we have to tolerate not knowing exactly which elements of our patients' narratives are objectively accurate in detail and which elements have been distorted by the context of the original experience or the context of the recalling. Indeed, one of our key therapeutic tasks may be to help our patients tolerate that same uncertainty.

No pre-trauma psychic structure

For many years psychoanalytic literature has directed its attention away from the external act and focused primarily, or even exclusively, on the patient's internal world. This reflects Freud's own shift of emphasis from 1896 onwards. In directing our attention away from external reality and focusing on internal reality, it is held that traumatic experiences are experienced as traumatic because they become archaic representations of whatever was frightening and so lead to an overflow of excitation (e.g. Garland, 2002; Levy & Lemma, 2004). However, in this regard there is an important difference between trauma experienced in later childhood and adulthood, and trauma beginning in infancy, such as that experienced by most people with DID. In an older person, the effect of trauma will be determined by the psychic structures already in place, which in turn will be partly the result of constitutional factors and partly the result of our early experiences, especially experiences with our caregivers (Bowlby, 1969, 1973; Winnicott, 1965, 1971). In the case of infant trauma that was ongoing and severe and perhaps inflicted by caregivers, the traumatic experience itself will have had a major formative effect on the emerging psychic structure. Indeed, it is widely agreed that a diagnosis of DID is *prima facie* evidence of early trauma, because only severe disruption before the sense of self as an individual is formed can produce such severe dissociative symptoms.

For this reason, psychotherapy work with a person with DID that focuses on the pre-trauma psychic structures that have shaped their response to trauma is seeking to do the impossible, because in the case of infant trauma there was, in one sense, no pre-trauma psychic structure. Such therapy is in danger of focusing on the person's internal reality at the expense of ignoring the formative effect of external reality. Addressing the external environmental reality must be a key part of the therapy.

Presentation that facilitates disbelief

When a patient with DID tells about an experience of abuse, it is not unusual for another personality to subsequently deny or contradict the account given. This denying personality may be correct in asserting that the event did not take place, or may just have no knowledge that the abusive experience occurred, or may be motivated by loyalty to the abusers, or may be terrified of being punished if the abuse is disclosed, or may simply be scared of being disbelieved.

Some people with DID present their narratives of sadistic abuse in a quite matter-of-fact way, without perceptible affect. This may sometimes be done as a way of protecting themselves, and the listener, from the emotional impact of their experience. We have found that people describing trauma in a flat way, without feeling, are usually those who have been more chronically abused, while those with affect still have a sense of self that can observe the tragedy of betrayal and have feelings about it. In some cases, this deadpan presentation can also be the result of cult training and brainwashing. Unfortunately, when a patient describes a traumatic experience without showing any apparent emotion, it can make the listener doubt whether the patient is telling the truth.

A therapist can also experience a countertransference of disbelief when the patient has internalized a very specific combined object (Valerie Sinason, personal communication). The child cries out for help to an attachment figure and receives a discrediting, disconfirming response. The child introjects this combination—a cry that is disconfirmed—and through that grows up with multiple enactments of the same scenario, a cry that is always ignored. Through this the child achieves loyalty and identification with a disconfirming object. As an adult, she presents her experience in a way that remains loyal to the original caregiver/abuser by unconsciously facilitating a re-enactment of disbelief by the therapist.

Disbelief from the therapist can actually lead a patient to develop a truthful account into a fabricated account, with or without the patient's conscious intention. When a patient correctly senses that a therapist does not believe his or her truthful account, the patient can then sometimes unconsciously fabricate details because this makes him or her angrily in control of further rejection (Hale & Sinason, 1994). The patient was not in control of the original abuse he or she experienced, and it is important for the patient's psychic survival that he or she does not place him/herself in a similar vulnerable situation of being hurt again by the therapist's disbelief; better to be in control of that anticipated rejection by his or her own action of fabrication. Whether this mechanism is conscious or unconscious, it can leave the patient not knowing what is true or not.

In cases of organized and multi-perpetrator abuse when the abuse occurs in the context of rituals and ceremonies, some elements of the experience may have been staged specifically with the intention of encouraging the disbelief of others if the victim were to report the crime. For example, someone reporting such a crime may mention that the devil was present, or that someone well-known was there, or that acts of magic were performed. These were tricks and deceptions by the abusers—often experienced by the victims after being given medication or hallucinogenic drugs—that render the account unbelievable, make the witness sound unreliable, and protect the perpetrators.

Disbelief as a defence

When a therapist hears an account of severe abuse, there can be an understandable wish to avoid an uncomfortable objective truth. Such cruel and criminal actions, especially those involving children, seriously challenge the common assumption that in our society criminality and cruelty are moderated; if people do truly appalling things to other people, this happens only in other countries, or other cultures, or happened a long time ago. Sometimes, as therapists, it is only after we have worked through our initial feelings of nausea and disbelief that we are able to realize that we were initially avoiding knowledge of the abuse because we were unable to tolerate the possibility of its occurring, a process discussed by Bowlby (1988) and Laub and Auerhahn (1993).

Faced with our own anxiety at our helplessness in the face of the horrific crimes committed against our patient, perhaps one way therapists manage that anxiety, and feel less helpless, is by questioning the truth of our patient's account. Disbelief can also help us avoid a moral responsibility to take action, such as reporting the crime. If we believe these accounts of dreadful crimes, are we not morally obliged to do something? Perhaps we excuse our failure to act by defensive denial—holding in mind that what our patient is telling us might not be true. Sometimes we may even feel the impulse to make this explicit by using the adjective *alleged* to describe the crimes reported by our patients with DID.

In everyday life, we routinely believe what other people tell us, and expect them to believe what we tell them, without proof being needed. When we use the word *alleged*, it carries enormous emotional meaning. Ninety-nine per cent of human life exists without putting the word *alleged* in front of it. However, as soon as some sorts of crime are mentioned in the consulting room, it can feel that the discussion has entered the legal domain and clinicians can get scared of saying the wrong thing and being in trouble. There can be a fear of ending up in a court of law and being prosecuted or sued. There can also be a fear of being accused by colleagues and others of being gullible. It can feel more professional to use the legal qualifier *alleged*, even though it may not occur to us to use it when naming other crimes mentioned in the consulting room. We should be aware that we are borrowing the word from a different profession, one that practises in a different context—the justice system—in which things are either proven or not proven and the distinction must be made in order to distinguish between them. In contrast, in our profession of psychotherapy everything we hear in the consulting room is unproven, so to label some clinical material *alleged* implies a false distinction from other clinical material.

The impact of belief and disbelief

Given that we cannot know which clinical material is historically true or not true, our expressions of belief or disbelief should be guided by what is clinically helpful. The prevailing view among psychoanalytic psychotherapists is that it is important to maintain as neutral a stance as possible in relation to the patient's material by neither validating nor invalidating the patient's account. This very neutral stance by the therapist allows the patient the possibility of reading the therapist's attitude according to what the patient expects the therapist's attitude to be—that is, developing a transference relationship with the therapist that is based on the patient's earlier experiences with others. The work of the therapy is then to recognize and work through this transference. All patients will find at times that a very neutral stance from their psychotherapist feels hostile. However, with the help of the therapist, they are generally able to tolerate and work through those negative feelings and move forward in the therapy. Indeed, some psychotherapists would argue that it is only by a patient experiencing and working through the anxiety generated by a neutral stance that real psychic change can occur.

Such an approach can be very effective with non-traumatized patients; however, more severely traumatized patients need a modified approach that remains psychoanalytically informed but takes account of the high levels of chronic anxiety in this group. This is especially true for patients who have been severely abused, because they are likely to experience a non-supportive stance as disbelieving and hostile to a degree that cannot be tolerated, and the therapy is likely to break down.

Maria

Maria was 32 years old and suffering from DID when she came into therapy. She had been severely sexually abused from birth and had developed a number of personalities to take the abuse in order that it could be kept out of her day-to-day awareness. Her abuse ended when she went to university. Once Maria was out of the abuse, the personalities that had been created to take the abuse remained dormant, and she had no knowledge of them, nor of what had been done to her. She was in her late twenties when her parents died within a few months of each other. Maria then had a major depressive episode, accompanied by increasing flashbacks of the abuse and periods of what initially appeared to be regression, which required hospitalization. Fortunately, her psychiatrist at the hospital correctly diagnosed DID. She began psychotherapy with a thoughtful and experienced therapist. However, this therapy broke down after a few months because her therapist said to her, "We have to keep an open mind about what you are remembering." This was understood by the child person-alities as meaning that they were not telling the truth, which was experienced as a re-enactment of being called a liar when she tried to report the abuse as a child. The therapy continued for a while, but the child personalities no longer spoke to the therapist, and the therapy broke down.

Amy

Amy was in her forties and had already had several years of successful psychotherapy when her elderly therapist began to plan for her retirement. Amy's DID had been resolved unusu-ally quickly early in the therapy, and for some years most of the work in the therapy sessions consisted of exploring the severe here-and-now emotional deficits that were the sequelae of Amy's long history of chronic sexual abuse. Amy was given twelve months' notice of her therapist's retirement, and it was decided by them both that Amy would continue the therapeu-tic work with a carefully chosen new therapist. After a short break, Amy began working with the new therapist, and for the first six months the weekly sessions were almost completely filled with Amy repeating her account of the abuse, which she could remember in graphic and horrific detail, which she had not discussed in therapy for several years. Any session time spent on other matters was devoted to describing in detail how she had been let down by the police and medical profession, issues that she had also not discussed in therapy recently. Amy repeated her account of these experiences many times and checked that the new therapist understood and believed her experience. Only after many months, when her new therapist had demonstrated a capacity to believe and to bear witness to her experiences, was Amy able to trust the therapist enough to return to the kind of work she had been doing with her previous therapist, which focused on her present-day emotional difficulties, both in the consulting room and in her day-to-day life, and on the links between these and her earlier experiences.

For both Maria and Amy the levels of anxiety and fear of disbelief were so high that a careful expression of belief by the psychotherapist was needed to justify the enormous risk involved in trusting and speaking.

Discussion

Telling the truth is often the last thing that severely abused people want to do, because it involves great risk. They risk disbelief, they may risk reprisals from their abusers for telling, and they may risk rejection by their abusers/caregivers, to whom they may have an ongoing attachment. In some cases, they may also have been perpetrators themselves, as well as victims, and so may risk prosecution themselves. For people with DID, there are likely to be inside personalities that are strongly opposed to telling others what was done to them. These may be terrified personalities who still believe the claims of their abusers that they will know if they tell anyone and that great harm will come them, or people they care for, if they speak of the abuse. Some personalities may think we could be an abuser and will hurt them for speaking. There may also be personalities who are loyal to the abusers, and these will have equally strong reasons to keep the abuse secret. They may fear that the psychotherapist will tell the police. It would feel much safer for these patients to keep quiet.

Many of our patients have encountered disbelief from the police and medical profession, and sometimes disbelief even earlier within their own family from an abusing caregiver who was seeking to deny the reality of the child's account in order to keep the crimes hidden, or from a non-abusing caregiver who could not bear to know an unbearable truth. One concrete way in which we all landscape our sanity is by having our experience of reality confirmed by others. When our experience of reality is disconfirmed by others, our confidence in our own sanity can be undermined. Let us imagine a young girl who is taken from her bed in the night by Mummy or Daddy, is sexually abused, and remembers it clearly, including being covered in blood. In the morning the child wakes up back in her own bed, between clean sheets, and the same Mummy or Daddy is kind to her and asks if she slept well. In the face of this disconfirmation of her experience, the child may come to doubt her own sanity. Some people with DID with whom I have worked have felt more abused by those who should have kept them safe but failed to do so—both family and professionals—than by those who committed the actual crimes. When a therapist expresses doubt about the truth of a patient's account, the patient experiences it as a re-enactment of these experiences of disbelief, and this re-enactment can be re-traumatizing.

When a therapist is aware of the risks that a patient with DID may be taking in speaking of the crimes committed against him or her, it can lead to a strong countertransferential pull to give the patient a response that tells him or her it was worth taking that risk. In formulating our therapeutic responses to such a patient, our challenge as therapists is to find a stance that is honourable both to the patient's experience and to our own uncertainty about exactly which elements of our patients' narratives are objectively accurate in detail.

Postscript

I began this chapter with David's question to me: did I think he was making this up? I did not interpret his question. I answered him with the words, "I believe that dreadful things were done to you. Maybe they happened exactly as you remember, maybe they've got a bit changed around in your memory, maybe they were even worse than you remember, but I don't think you're making this up." David said nothing, but his eyes filled with tears. Had my answer been therapeutic? Was it honourable both to his experience and to my own uncertainty? I hope so. I know that following this exchange, David's trust and confidence in the therapy grew, and we were able to continue our work together.

Infanticidal attachment: the link between dissociative identity disorder and crime

Adah Sachs

The *DSM–IV–TR* (APA, 2000) states that individuals with dissociative identity disorder (DID) frequently report having experienced severe physical and sexual abuse, especially during childhood.[1] Many authors have attempted to explain this link between abuse and dissociation. Schore (1994, 2003), Davies and Frawley (1994), van der Kolk, McFarlane, and Weisaeth (1996), Wilkinson (2006), and others have written extensively on the neurobiological process that leads from extreme trauma to dissociation, as a bodily "shutting-down" response. Ross (2000) describes a deliberate creation of DID through government-sponsored mind-control programs. Van der Hart, Nijenhuis, and Steele (2006) coin and describe *structural dissociation* as the result of chronic, especially (but not only) early, traumatization. Liotti (1999), Southgate (1996), Sinason (2002), and others have written about the link between trauma and dissociation from an attachment perspective, focusing on disorganized attachment as the almost inevitable sequel of severe relational trauma.

In this chapter, I would like to add to the attachment-based discussion regarding extreme relational trauma in infancy and its link to DID. I shall focus on the special role that *infanticidal attachment* (Kahr, 2007) plays in the most severe forms of dissociative disorders. And as infanticide—the practice of killing infants—is among the worst of crimes, I would emphasize the forensic aspects of the trauma in the lives of people with DID, and the special significance of this element.

Infanticidal attachment

> "Francine still believes that Daddy was trying to kill her, and if she'd been a good girl she would have stopped breathing and died. . . ."
>
> "i just have to lie really really quiet and still and see if am dead later."
>
> "Aahbee" (chapter 4)

The words "infanticidal attachment" are very evocative, which suggests that they are describing something that we can recognize. I would like to place this "something" in the context of the known attachment types.

Attachment, the term coined by John Bowlby (1958), is an innate structure in humans and animals that makes the young seek the proximity of a specific caregiver (the attachment-figure), for the purpose of safety and thus survival. I would now look at the different identified forms or types of this structure as occupying points along a continuum of effectiveness in achieving the purpose of safety.

Attachment types

Secure attachment provides a stable, organized structure, allowing for separation, exploration, and play and serving as a basis for the formation of future relationships. It thus supports short- as well as long-term survival.

More painful, but still functional structures are present with *insecure attachment*. There are two types—avoidant and ambivalent—and these represent specific deficiencies in the relationship with the attachment-figure and are likely to lead to varying degrees of difficulties in forming future intimate relationships (e.g. with partner, children). However, these insecurely attached babies were consistently able to reach the attachment-figure, although they had to go about it in a roundabout, painful way. Attachment behaviour of the kind that the parent could tolerate did prove effective, consistently producing the proximity, safety, and comfort needed. The attachment style that resulted was thus organized and stable, if not happy.

With *disorganized attachment* we move to the sphere of trauma. The baby never knows what would bring comfort or safety, as this is unpredictable. In the case of neglect, for example, the baby gets no comfort at all for lengthy periods, no matter what attachment behaviour is expressed. In the case of abuse, the confusion and terror are greater, as the attachment-figure, towards which the child turns in distress, is also the one causing the hurt. In the case of a mentally ill, depressed, or dissociative parent, there are so many variables affecting the parent's capacity to respond helpfully that no consistent way of reaching comfort can possibly be found, and the child is in a constant, frantic search for the parental closeness. Disorganized attachment, while reaching for safety, may also become a hindrance to it, by linking the infant to a figure that may be dangerous and by exposing him or her to further trauma.

Disorganized attachment is, statistically, the single most important predisposing factor for dissociative traits in adult life, from developing dissociative disorders to a high propensity for PTSD. It also predicts a much higher likelihood for psychiatric distress or for criminal activity (Hesse & Main, 2000).

So far there have been a few suggestions for subdividing the disorganized attachment classification.

Liotti (1999, 2006) talks about three motivational systems that could replace the painful experience of the disorganized attachment system being activated. He calls them the *agonistic, sexual, and caregiving* systems and explains that each of them provides a way of being close to the longed-for figure in a less painfully vulnerable, dependent way. The use of these systems in defensive replacement of the attachment system is expressed in three types of controlling strategies: punitive, sexualized, and caregiving. We may consider these controlling strategies as three more subtypes of disorganized attachment, as they fulfil the same role (immediate reduction of distress by achieving proximity to the attachment figure).

The category *cannot classify* in the Adult Attachment Interview (AAI) was suggested by Hesse (1996). This category is thought to be a more severe and pervasive form of the *disorganized* category, where the "disorganization" appears throughout the interview, and not just at specific, difficult points of it. One may speculate that this result may belong to people with DID.

In every case of disorganized attachment, the actual relationship between the attachment-figure and the infant is traumatic and traumatizing. Severe neglect, mental illness, and physical or sexual abuse cause unspeakable damage to the infant, *but they do not necessarily intend to cause damage.* These parents may well love and attempt to protect the baby when and where they can, despite the damage that they inflict at other times. One may say that these parents "take out on the baby" their own uncontainable emotions of aggression, despair, sexual arousal, or fear, unable to care, in these moments, for the baby's feelings or needs. It is as though the baby becomes, temporarily, invisible to the parent, not a real person.

Now let us consider the additional harm where *there is an intention, a wish, or actual attempts* to mutilate or kill the child. The child, in these cases, is not invisible: he or she is specifically targeted by the attachment-figure as a "chosen sacrifice" or as an object of hate, in fantasy or in practice. This, I suggest, is where *infanticidal attachment* will result. On our continuum of functionality, it is the most dysfunctional, as it increases, rather than reduces, the risk to the child's well-being or even life.

A child with an *infanticidal attachment type* (Kahr, 2007) feels reassured by, and thus strives for, the proximity of a murderous caregiver. This leaves the child completely exposed to further damage which emanates from the attachment-figure. As well as impacting on the child's safety, this also creates a particular kind of attachment-behaviour, which aims, as does all attachment-behaviour, to engage the caregiver. This type of attachment behaviour becomes apparent in the process of therapy of infanticidally attached people and represents a serious challenge to the therapy.

Infanticidal caregivers, however, vary in the quality and type as well as the intensity of their murderous feelings. I would therefore like to draw a distinction between two types of infanticidal states of mind, the *symbolic* and the *concrete*. Subsequently, I would distinguish *symbolic infanticidal attachment* from *concrete infanticidal attachment*. I suspect that only those infants who were exposed to the *concrete* type of infanticidal caregiving would develop DID, with all its distinctive features.

The spectrum of attachment types, in decreasing order of safety, can be summarized as follows:

SECURE

INSECURE

   Insecure avoidant / Insecure ambivalent

DISORGANIZED

   "Replacement": Agonistic / Sexualized / Caregiving   [Liotti]

   Cannot classify   [Hesse]

   Infanticidal attachment (IA)   [Kahr]

   Symbolic IA / Concrete IA   [Sachs]

Symbolic and concrete infanticidal attachment

While it appears that a large percentage of people with schizophrenia, as well as other mental disorders, have suffered parental infanticidal ideation or intentions (Kahr, 1994, 2007; Ross, 2004), I would like to emphasize the predominantly symbolic form that characterized these death threats. The symbolic form in which parental murderousness gets expressed shapes, as it always does, the attachment-behaviour of the baby and may lead to the highly symbolic language of schizophrenia (as well as some other forms of mental illness). The history of people with DID, on the other hand, seems to invariably include early exposure to parental concrete acts of murder or torture, which the infant endures, witnesses, or is forced to commit. This, I would argue, is a necessary condition for developing the concrete language of DID.

The parallels between the type of parental expression of murderousness and the attachment-language in the child (symbolic leads to symbolic, concrete leads to concrete) should hardly be surprising to us: attachment-behaviour—the "reaching-out" language of the baby—is always modulated by the language of the attachment-figure, as it aims to engage with the attachment-figure.[2]

While *symbolic infanticidal attachment* can occur due to a variety of tragic circumstances (Green, 1986; Hollins & Sinason, 2000; Sachs, 1997), I suggest that the *concrete type* will only occur where there are concrete, actual, intentional, and repeated torture and death threats at the hands of an attachment-figure. The diagnosis of DID, therefore, may have to be seen as a marker for forensic concern, as it is likely to indicate extreme childhood abuse, though not the identity of the abuser(s).

Attachment needs, however, cannot be "switched-off". An infant cannot forego having an attachment-figure, whatever the qualities of that figure may be. Furthermore, an infant's attachment-style will, inevitably, mimic the person to whom the infant is attached. If that person wants the baby dead or mutilated, the baby will become attached in that particular way: "Mum loves me when I'm screaming in pain. Dad will be with me if I'm good and dead." The baby's feeling of comfort will thus be linked to death, hate, or sadistic thrill in the same way that it is linked to being distant if their parent is AAI *dismissive* type. The sight of torture will be linked to the feeling of safety or even love, in the same way that the sound of a mother's voice singing a lullaby is linked to it.

I suggest that the term *infanticidal attachment*, symbolic or concrete, would correctly fit the attachment-style of babies whose parents are not just unable to contain their aggression or despair, but who actively want or need to see them dead or mutilated, whether they imply that wish or act on it.

It goes without saying that parents who feel compelled to see their children tortured or dead have an extremely traumatic history themselves. And it is the inevitability of further trauma, generation after generation, that makes it so critically important to offer therapy to persons of any age who present with this type of attachment-style.

Clinical examples

A child who is attached to an infanticidal caregiver experiences reduction of stress when he or she is in the proximity of a person who aims to torture or kill them. This attachment further exposes the child to danger, with no way of abating it. It is thus dangerous, as well as traumatizing. I would now like to draw a distinction between infanticidal ideation or intentions that are symbolically implied and those that are concretely acted upon. The severity of either can vary, but, to my mind, there is a qualitative, not just quantitative, difference between them.

The following are short examples that may serve to illustrate the difference between symbolic and concrete parental murderousness:

Christina, a young woman with schizophrenia, said she was named after Christ because she had to die for the sins of others. She knew that she really was Christ, because she could walk through walls; in fact, she was compelled to walk through walls, explaining that if she was only allowed to do so, "peace will come to earth, and all the sins will be forgotten." Naturally, hospital staff were not in favour of this behaviour, as she had already broken her nose and a knee-cap in these attempts.

Christina was conceived when her mother had an affair with a married man. The man didn't want to leave his wife, and Christina's mother, who was Catholic, could not have an abortion. She married another man, whom she didn't love, and had a very unhappy marriage. Christina felt she really should have died, "walked through the wall" of her mother's womb, and then her mother's sin would have been "forgotten". Instead, they all lived very unhappily together.

The infanticidal ideation that the mother may well have entertained had never been acted on but was implied in a hundred ways—for one, by telling this story to Christina as soon as she reached puberty, as a warning. She never had any other children, saying that "more children would kill her". Mother and Christina were very close and "had their own [symbolic] language", having this big secret to keep.

Christina's language was equally symbolic: she was Christ, because she was to die for the sin of her mother, and she had to walk through walls—that is, not have a physical body—in order to bring peace to earth. In the therapy, much of the work was to do with me having to find the meaning of each symbol, in answer to her desperate plea for being liberated from the deadly secret.

Emma, by contrast, had a completely different language and a different trauma history. Aged 15, she was an extremely ill patient whose self-harm behaviour was particularly dangerous. We knew that she had been badly abused as a young child, but she never revealed any details of the abuse, the identity of the abusers, or, in particular, the way in which they used to get hold of her each time. Emma communicated mostly through drawings, and a few written words. She hardly talked. In her art therapy sessions, she repeatedly produced images of many *arms* reaching to grab a little person who was chained to a table, and of a *key*. The art therapist and myself tried for months to follow her line of communication, expecting the *arms* images to be the *key* to the riddle of the people who harmed her. In other words, we understood the images of the key to have the symbolic meaning of *key*—that is, a *clue*. But we were wrong. Emma kept producing the same images, and to all our explorations of hidden clues she answered a definite "No".

The breakthrough happened one day when, despairing of ever "getting it", I asked Emma "was there a real key there?" She looked at me with relief and nodded "yes". Emma herself, under threats, had given the abusers a key for the back door of the house. It was not a symbol, but a straightforward, concrete description of the way the abuse could take place.

Jo, a terribly thin and grubby young man, used to tell me extremely lengthy stories involving his visits to ancient Egypt, where he was the king's hieroglyphics writer and lived in the City of the Dead. He was a professional translator of eight languages, when he wasn't in psychiatric admissions, and an interpreter of dreams for the ward when he was in hospital. He always told me that I'll get nowhere without "learning the secrets first". The secrets, of course, were not about the Egyptian Royal Court but about the home that he grow up in, "the City of the Dead", where his father, the king, didn't want any children (the Pharaoh who put to death all the Israelites' first-born?). Father was 15 years younger than mother and had always maintained that he, father, "needed her more than anyone".

Here, too, the symbolic language of hiding the truth that was used by the whole family could be seen in Jo's highly symbolic, schizophrenic language.

The "young Virginia Woolf" (Lidz, 1973, quoted in Kahr, 2007) could serve as another example of symbolic infanticidal attachment. She was a schizophrenic patient of Lidz, and I have named her "the young Virginia Woolf" because her mother, who adored the famous author, regularly likened her daughter to her in talent and in personality. The girl, tragically, ended up committing suicide. We may suspect that the nature of her attachment to her mother was infanticidal, which may have been the reason for her tragic death. The quality of the infanticidal attachment was symbolic: for all we know, the mother had never attempted to kill the girl or hurt her. On the contrary, she rather idealized her daughter as being of a rare literary talent and sophistication. One had to know the life (and death) story of Virginia Woolf to see the significance and intensity of the mother's message to the girl: "I'll love you best when you're dead."

Jane, aged 15, by contrast, told me a lot of stories about the pets that had died in their house, and how upset she was when the man in the pet shop, to whom she went for advice, tried to comfort her by saying that "these things just happened". She went on to tell me the details of how the dog bit her because he was scared, because the pet rat had bitten him, and that the pet rat was missing some toes and was bleeding.

Jane was brought to hospital in her parents' arms, literally dying. Her bodyweight was at 50% of normal, a level of starvation from which recovery is rare in medical literature. The obvious question—why did the parents wait so long before seeking help—was not answered, but it is hard to miss the infanticidal intention of such a lack of action. She was not psychotic, and, I'd add, not symbolic. She was a survivor of ritual abuse, in a family where children were made to cut, kill, and eat body parts of animals from an early age, as part of their "training". Her stories about the dead and mutilated animals were not, as I first suspected, a symbolic description of her own self-hatred and death-wish. She did not want to die. She wanted someone to notice what was *actually* happening at home; hence her upset about her unsatisfactory "consultation" with the man in the pet shop. What she told me was a concrete description of actual events, and her refusal to eat was her revulsion at being forced to ingest the body parts of her pets. Her story had a partial corroboration.

Discussion

I suggest that what differentiates these cases from one another is that in the "concrete infanticidal attachment" group (Emma and Jane) the infanticidal ideation was not covert, not implied, not hidden, not symbolized. It was acted upon, as though there was nothing to hide or to cover. What is grossly forensic, and thus normally hidden, was simply allocated to another, "not-me" part of the self (both in the parent and in the infant), and therefore did not need to find a complex way to be "lived with" or integrated.

Christina, "the young Virginia Woolf", and Jo, on the other hand, came from families who symbolized their murderous feelings and expressed them in a way that made them almost unnoticed. The three young people that I have described similarly expressed their fears and anguish in symbolic, complex ways that made them appear rather mad, but did not expose (even to themselves) the murderousness of their attachment-figures.

It is my experience that people with DID are remarkably literal. When they draw a baby they mean a baby, not a representation of a needy part of the self; when they say a knife they mean a knife, not a representation of danger or sexuality. When they say "I cannot talk to you about these things" it is because they were "trained" or brainwashed not to be able to betray secrets, which made them literally not able to do so, rather than embarrassed to discuss a shameful topic. Often, when their accounts seemed totally implausible to me, I have tried to find an alternative explanation that could make sense of what they have said. Almost invariably, I have subsequently learned that the account was literal and accurate, if not complete. And the missing information was due to dissociation, either spontaneous or induced, and not to elaboration of the truth. We may say that these stories are quite simple and single-layered in their meaning: Jane was afraid of being forced to actually kill her pets and eat parts of their bodies, and this is what she tried to express. Her stories about frightened, dead, and mutilated animals, as well as her severe anorexia, were like a trail of breadcrumbs leading to the truth: whispered, but not symbolized.

Conversely, the symbolic type of infanticidal attachment produces "nameless dread" (Bion, 1967). Because the reason for the fear—namely, the infanticidal intention of the caregiver—was covert, hidden, symbolized, the dread was detached from its "name", from its cause. Jo was terrified of a king in the City of the Dead, not of Dad. Lidz's patient, if the analysis is correct, went to the nth degree in trying to appease her infanticidal mother, who loved Virginia Woolf. None of the infanticidal ideation or wishes was directly expressed. Subsequently, all the terror got expressed by the child (and later, the adult) in that same covert, hidden, symbolic way, which protected everyone from knowing about the parental murderousness.

Making the division between the symbolic and the concrete may help our understanding of dissociation on the attachment map, but it has another, far more uncomfortable aspect. It states a difference between the tragic damage done to a child through their attachment to a person with infanticidal ideation (symbolic type), to the criminal damage done to a child through their attachment to a person or a group who openly act in a murderous way (concrete type). For the therapist, this represents a new level of challenge, as the forensic becomes a centrepiece in the therapeutic process.

It is important to stress that while I have stated that there must have been an actual, intended, and murderous abuse in the background of anyone with DID, and that the abuser(s) must be the victim's attachment-figure(s), this does not necessarily help to identify the perpetrators. In many such cases, the abusive attachment-figure is a group, rather than an individual. Such a group has a whole hierarchy of people involved in abusing children, while "training" them to become part of the group. Furthermore, when one is in the grip of extreme terror or pain, the people who inflict it or stop it can become new attachment-figures, even at a later age. Identifying this type of attachment thus tells us that something awful was done to a person; but it is still a far cry from knowing what was done, how, or by whom. And it is even a further cry from being able to stop it, or to bring about healing.

A brief word about healing, the ultimate aim of all our attempts to understand. Becker and Karriker (private communication, 2007), as part of the Extreme Abuse Surveys, explored the views of survivors on the helpfulness of 53 healing methods. The preliminary results of the survey show that the three methods that were marked "great help" most frequently were individual psychotherapy, personal prayer, and supportive friends. From an attachment perspective, it is notable that all three involve closeness, and someone listening. Poignantly, it seems as though what helps to heal the damage of a murderous attachment is a benign and deep relatedness.

Notes

1. This finding is further elaborated in the writing of Davies and Frawley (1994), Mollon (1996, 1998), van der Kolk, McFarlane, and Weisaeth (1996), van der Hart, Nijenhuis, and Steele (2006), Ross (2000, 2004), Schore (1994, 2003), Sinason (1994, 1998, 2002), and others. Quantitative studies are offered by Ross (2004), who links DID to "a history of *particularly severe* childhood trauma" (emphasis added), demonstrating the very high proportion of such trauma in

this group in a large number of independent studies. Becker, Karriker, Over-kamp, and Rutz (chapter 3) report preliminary results that reflect a sample of over 2,000 survivors and professionals from 40 countries. The authors show a very high correlation between DID and a list of abuse types, all of which are extreme.

2. Hollins and Sinason (2000) point out the risk of disorganized attach-ment and death-wishes in some people with learning disabilities, who could sense the wishes of their attachment-figure for them to have been aborted.

CHAPTER ELEVEN

Letter from a general practitioner

Alison Anderson

Adah Sachs and Graeme Galton
Consultant Psychotherapists
Clinic for Dissociative Studies
London

Dear Adah and Graeme,

I would appreciate the opportunity to share my thoughts about some clinical issues regarding the treatment of the patient that we share, who has dissociative identity disorder.

Perhaps it would be helpful if I gave you some of the background. I had been Katie's GP for several years and had known her as a quite regular attender—an unhappy woman of about 40, with recurrent depression and intermittent contact with the Community Mental Health Team. There had been a few attempted overdoses in the past, and a suggestion of some sort of personality

---

This letter is published with the permission of the patient. Identifying details have been changed. *Eds.*

disorder, never finalized. She was on several different medications, some for depression, some for chronic pain, and one day as I was asking Katie how she was, she said, in a rather different voice, "Actually, it's Kielly."

And so I entered into the confusing world of DID. At times it feels like a Hitchcock story rather than an actual medical condition, and, for the GP, the almost constant underlying feeling is that you are joining and possibly increasing your patient's delusion, rather than helping and treating a very difficult psychological condition. This is largely because DID is barely mentioned in medical school, and I have never read an article on it in the usual GP journals. Most GPs, when confronted with such a diagnosis, have very little recourse to informed colleagues, and very few have even heard about it, let alone understand the condition.

My subsequent research into DID quickly showed me what a challenging condition it is to treat. I was aware that Katie had had a dreadfully abusive childhood, with physical, emotional, and sexual abuse occurring on a regular basis, at times involving satanic rituals. During such torment, I learned, individuals may shut themselves off from the pain by "creating" another personality who suffers the abuse in their stead, allowing them to close off the memories and try to live as normally as possible. Unfortunately for Katie, this had occurred countless times, and now there were tens of different "personalities" in her "system".

I found it a difficult concept to understand, and yet, at times, in medicine one has to suspend disbelief and go with the flow, if it seems that this explanation, for the time being at least, will lead to further understanding of and help for the patient.

A huge initial problem for me, quite apart from trying to understand this for myself, was the fact that the local mental health team, including the consultant psychiatrist, did not appear to understand or believe in this condition. It was suggested by the team that Katie would see a psychologist—but the only one available was male, and Katie was quite unable to open up to a male therapist, having been repeatedly abused by male family members whom she had previously trusted. It was at this point that I learned of your Clinic as a specialist DID service in London. I could hardly believe that there were people out there who specialized in this!

We then began the battle for "out-of-area" funding with the local Primary Care Trust. If I did not know much about DID before, it was not surprising that the non-medics in charge of funding out-of-area treatments would not have heard of it. Eventually, however, they agreed to pay for Katie to have a comprehensive assessment for a dissociative disorder, and treatment finally got under way, over a year after Kielly had announced herself.

Of course, despite my relief that Katie was now getting specialist help for a condition that I now believed existed but frankly didn't understand, there were other issues along the way.

For example, one day Katie came to see me because she wanted to tell me she had been raped and needed me to know, as her GP. Although Katie knew this was difficult to prove physically, as she had not been able to come sooner or keep the clothes as evidence, she still felt it important for this evil deed to be recorded by someone she trusted and knew would believe her. Now, the normal process in this situation would be to counsel the victim and encourage the person to go to the police to report the rape. However, I was aware that Katie had been put in this situation by those personalities who feel they still need to stay loyal to their cult families to keep themselves safe, yet unknowingly put Katie in more danger. I could just imagine how a police officer might react to this story—probably thinking that Katie was quite mad—and of course a conviction in court would be quite impossible. So what to do?

This is the sort of problem arising for the GP of a patient with this difficult condition. Thankfully, Katie's counsellor had already taken her to the police, who were way ahead of me on this one. Sadly, perhaps they have already seen other young women with this terrible condition.

Due to the satanic nature of the abuse, there are particular times of the year when Katie needs extra help: the summer and winter solstices, Halloween, and Good Friday in particular. At times, we have needed to find a place of safety for her, from which her family and other members of the cult could not find her. This has been very challenging and difficult as the "normal channels" were not really suitable. It is very hard for anyone to achieve a psychiatric admission nowadays, as a visiting specialist team often cares for even the actively suicidal at home rather than admitting them to hospital, and so this has been an area in which we have often needed to rely on private charitable institutions in order to provide inpatient respite care.

Another problem is that Katie has a medical problem that requires intermittent blood tests. Due to some of the dreadful abuse, involving needles and other implements of torture, it is very hard to get Katie to consent to anything that might constitute an invasion of her body. However, Kielly is much calmer about these things, so one finds oneself in the unusual situation of trying to ask Kielly to "come up" for the blood test, and then for Katie to return to discuss the result!

As time goes on, I have learned to recognize three of Katie's personalities even as she comes through the door—it is hard to explain exactly how. There are slight differences in her walk, the way her eyes meet yours, and certainly in her voice. So if I say "Hello, Kielly" or "Hello, Nikki", she is surprised and pleased to be recognized. But then again, the seed of doubt is always just below the surface. Is this helping Katie or harming her? After all, is not the therapist's ultimate aim to merge all these personalities so that Katie is just Katie?

Actually, I am not sure; one of the many things that I am unsure about in this condition. With so very little (almost nothing) written about this in GP literature—nothing helpful in understanding management, anyway—I often feel as if I am groping forwards in the dark, learning along with Katie how to manage, how best to help.

It does seem, however, that over the past few years Katie is, in fact, gradually improving. At least there are far fewer episodes from which she emerges having no memory of what may have occurred during the preceding time period (often a sign that one of the destructive personalities had taken over), and she has managed to come off some of her medication. But the emotional cost to her has been high, as she had to recall some truly horrendous moments in her past in the process. I have found that my main role as her GP has been simply to be there, someone who believes in the problem but yet somewhat outside the solution, however ready to help, especially with physical problems. Just being able to say, "Actually, it's Kielly today, Katie hasn't been too well lately", is apparently a huge relief to her.

Katie's future is uncertain, but as her GP, I will be there for her each step of the way. And interestingly, I am now beginning to wonder about another patient who at times seems a completely different personality to her "normal self". This woman, also around age 40, also suffered sexual abuse in her past and lives in a difficult home situation. Will I dare to say anything? And if so, what will I say? "Who am I talking to today?" Perhaps. Or perhaps not.

Would that be opening up Pandora's box? Is Katie really happier now after years of therapy, with all these personalities openly competing inside her? Furthermore, do you think I have joined my patient's delusions? For many doctors, that question will always be there, hovering somewhere in the background.

Yours sincerely,

Alison Anderson
General Practitioner

CHAPTER TWELVE

Corroboration in the body tissues

John Silverstone

Before training in osteopathy, I obtained a degree in physiology, then trained and worked for 12 years in general nursing. I have been a qualified osteopath for 22 years, and in my work as an osteopath I have treated 10 patients with dissociative identity disorder. All my patients with DID reported injuries of various kinds that were inflicted by others. Some of these were physical injuries, including many childhood injuries, such as being picked up and thrown across a room, having their head banged against a wall, or being held by one arm and swung against a wall. Other injuries were current and were the result of ongoing abuse. These injuries included being hit hard over the vertex of the head with a heavy object, leaving a tissue memory of impaction of the upper cervical spine into its articulation close to the anterior margin of the foramen magnum, and being kicked in the lower posterior rib cage with resulting haematuria and hospitalization due to puncture of the kidney by fractured eleventh and twelfth ribs and crush fractures of the vertebral bodies at the thoraco-lumbar junction, necessitating hospitalization and fitting of a spinal brace. One patient reported being kept in extreme confinement locked in a cage, unable to stand up straight, or lie down, or stretch their limbs to full length. At some point in their treatment, all these patients reported sexual abuse.

It was distressing to deal with cases in which it was clear that the abuse was ongoing, also to deal with cases where the abuse left no physical scars. Examples included hearing that the clients had been held below the surface of a fluid until they thought they had drowned or that they had been temporarily buried in a coffin. Although there may be no physical scars, this abuse still leaves some form of tissue memory. The more abuse a patient has suffered, the harder it is to distinguish individual assaults. In these cases there is a cumulative effect of multiple injuries.

Credibility of the histories and evidence from patients' bodies

Some of the stories told by my patients with DID were initially hard to believe—for example, the stories of being caged or nearly being drowned. In these cases, I distinguish between taking the history from the patient and gathering information from a physical examination. In the cases that challenge credibility and leave no immediately visible physical scars, such as being caged, there are chronic fibrotic changes in the postural muscles as a result of not having been able to straighten up. This is accompanied by ligamentous shortening and restriction in the movements of the joints. This quality of muscle tissue and of motion might be expected in a 70-year-old but not in a 30-year-old, and it gives supporting evidence for the patient's stories.

With a straightforward physical injury, the palpatory qualities often enable the practitioner to determine the patient's age when he or she suffered it, even back to birth. With a high degree of practitioner reproducibility, it is possible to localize the date of an injury to within about five years, even in a 70-year-old, and to be more specific in a younger patient. If a patient comes to me with strange injuries that they maintain they suffered 20 years earlier, it may well be possible to say that the injuries are in fact more recent or the result of continuing abuse. The signs would include acute inflammation and muscle "spasms", which would be obvious to anyone used to dealing with injuries. Discerning whether there has been a fresh injury on top of an old one depends on whether the new injury happened the day before examination or two weeks earlier; the longer ago, the harder it is to tell. There was one occasion when a patient had been assaulted a couple of days earlier, and I was able to describe the injuries without being told of the assault. On that occasion the patient had certainly suffered multiple injuries. I give further examples below of patients whose bodies confirmed their story, which at first seemed unbelievable.

One important point is that I do not always tell people what I find in a physical examination, because I need to know that the DID personality I am currently talking to can bear knowing about experiences that he or she might be learning of for the first time. I need also to hold in mind whether it is an appropriate point in their therapy to receive such information and whether it may be a difficult time of year for a ritually abused patient, who is likely to be particularly sensitive around certain dates.

The osteopath and the psychotherapist need to work together, and I sometimes have to hold back my treatment when personalities appear that do not know the psychotherapist who is treating the patient. I am reluctant to do work that would uncover a plethora of psychological implications if the patient is not due to see his or her therapist for another week.

Tissue memory

I am aware that some people will find it hard to comprehend a therapeutic system—osteopathy—that functions by making an association between the living qualities of body tissues and their structural relationships. Imposed strains and altered relationships may be identified and dealt with utilizing either a structural or a qualitative approach, or both.

The location of impact, direction, degree of force, and duration of physical insult and response to it may all be discernible in the patient's tissues as what osteopathic practitioners term a tissue memory. There was one patient with DID whom I asked whether she had ever had an abortion. In fact, she had, although she had not told me. It is hard to explain the exact palpatory qualities that communicate how I had picked this up in her body tissues, in the same way that it is hard to explain the beauty of a flower to someone who is blind. If this seems exclusive—to be able to "see" in a palpatory manner—it is no more than the development of any physical skill. The neurological capacity to make amazing origami is available to most people, but few learn the skill. The mental subtlety to hear the question or statement that lies behind the words of a patient is a skill that takes time to develop. Twenty years ago, even ten years ago, I dismissed out of hand as being imaginary and nonsensical the same palpatory facilities that I now use every day. Every change that happens to a body—whether hormonal, emotional, or metabolic—leaves a characteristic tissue quality. So does anything that leaves an element of guilt, regret, or fear. The possibility of having a baby and then not doing so, especially if she had no freedom to choose, touches something deeply rooted in a woman's psyche and leaves a mark in the tissues. In the instance of abortion as above, palpation at some near but relatively non-threatening site, such as the knees (of the clothed patient), drew my attention to the traumatic state of the pelvic floor and the emotional qualities of that trauma—qualities that immediately brought to mind the instance of unwanted imposed abortion.

There was another example of a perfectly healthy woman, a recent postpartum mother, but not a DID patient, who was having difficulty resolving neck problems. She had had an abortion eight years earlier when in an unstable relationship. It was clear from her tissue quality that her feelings about the abortion were preventing resolution of her current neck problem. Without any suggestion of questioning the motivation or judgement of the woman in her decision to have that abortion, she was simply invited to express how she now felt about that event. Letting her express her emotions about that experience enabled the tissues to relax and facilitated an effective response to treatment.

Injuries to a patient with DID
that may be personality-specific

Some patients with DID tell me a lot of their history; others may want to hide it and do not tell me much of their history. For some of them, the only way they can cope is by not facing the pain they have endured or are currently enduring. Sometimes the personality giving the history simply does not know all of the more major traumas suffered. When I begin to inquire about their current physical condition, I can sometimes see them weakening because my questions about their pain focus their attention on feelings they do not want to acknowledge. Acknowledging pain has the effect of making the DID sufferer susceptible to the emergence of less capable personalities. I have had three or four cases where there were overt personality changes when specific parts of their body were touched during the course of treatment, and these switches of personality happened consistently when that part of the body was touched. It might have been contact with the angle of the second and third ribs on the left that would cause a child personality to emerge, or contact with the twelfth rib on the right that would cause the emergence of an adult artistic personality.

It is not uncommon for the trauma identified by palpatory information gathering to be personality-specific. One patient had been maltreated as a child by being swung by an arm against a wall so that the head hit the wall as a glancing blow. Unsurprisingly, I had found clear palpatory evidence for this trauma—in the child personality that received the abuse—before she told me. The wall had impacted the patient's head from behind as she was swung backward and off her feet through an arc that reached just beyond the limit imposed by the wall. The resulting impact caused a shear between the outermost part of the head where the ear is positioned and the rest of the skull and was retained as a tissue memory. The external ear sits over the temporal bone, and much of the articulation of the temporal bone with the vault of the skull takes the form of a very shallow bevel. In this patient the palpatory impression was that the position of the temporal bone relative to its surrounding bones was strained anteriorly within this shallow bevel because the side of the back of the head encountered the wall first. When the personality that received this injury was accessed during treatment, the tissue memory of that specific trauma was expressed.

Why does the body behave in this way, to relate specific tissue memories to specific personalities? There are documented accounts where the recipients of organ transplants have experienced changes of personality, changes of creative directions, changes of likes and dislikes, and even new specific memories following the transplant. Such personality traits and memories were unfamiliar to the transplant recipient, even totally foreign, but were characteristic of the donor. This transmission via transplant suggests that the brain is not the only seat of personality and memory. The idea that organs hold specific memory of life incidents is not at all foreign to me, because it is often the subject of clinical discussion between osteopaths. Reports of such palpatory impressions are commonplace and bear remarkable observer-consistency. One example is the impression that there is a complete locking down and closing up of the normal cranial rhythm in the pelvis of a child who has suffered sexual abuse, even if he or she is now adult.

In a case not involving DID, I found that memories of anger and distress "shouted" at me from the upper thorax of a young mother three years after she had a car accident in which a speeding car swung around the bend of a country lane directly towards her on the wrong side of the road. Fortunately, in the resulting head-on collision, her young daughter, who was strapped into the child seat beside her, was not injured. However, the mother's moment of reactive protection and maternal fury at the driver who put her child at risk had never been resolved. Thus, a trauma memory can be tissue- or organ-specific and associated with a specific incident. In a patient with DID, where that trauma occurred to a particular personality in childhood and is locked into some specific tissue reaction or a specific injury, then perhaps it will appear only when that personality is in current conscious focus.

Perhaps the question should not be: *Why* does the body behave in this way? We need to acknowledge that there is a large proportion of the nervous system about which, as yet, so little is understood and which has strong links with the limbic system, affecting mood, hormonal balance, perception, and so forth. Perhaps in this we can discover part of the reason for *how* the body behaves in this manner.

Use of osteopathic diagnosis as forensic evidence

It is interesting to consider whether my work could be used as forensic evidence and to compare it with that of police pathologists. It is not straightforward to use tissue memory as evidence because it is too subtle to show up in an MRI scan or an x-ray. Nonetheless, if five suitably experienced osteopaths independently examined the same patient, experience to date suggests that they would all find the same signs and that this should be convincing as forensic evidence. Of course, it would important for each osteopath to examine without treating (i.e. without influencing the tissue state), which is difficult. It would probably be more appropriate to assemble the practitioners to assess palpatory qualities concurrently.

Whether to report injuries

My first patient with DID came to me as a result of a phone call from a psychotherapist whom I did not know, who warned me about the possible appearance of different personalities in the patient. As I had previously dealt with schizophrenics in hospital as a nurse, I was not concerned if it suited a patient to pretend to be someone else. However, as I treated this patient and the level of trust increased, I became aware over a period of weeks or months that although the history recounted by the patient was grotesque, it fitted with the injuries. Moreover, each of the personalities had obvious integrity and consistency of expression in him/herself. That is to say, each personality behaved in a manner consistent with his or her previous expression of personality and with consistent truthfulness.

That first patient had more than 67 personalities. After treating her for several months, it became clear that she was subject to continuing abuse. It was staring me in the face that, after treatment, this person would go back to her own living environment and would suffer more abuse. Thus I started to become aware of landmarks in the year—certain dates—when her abuse would become more intense.

In conversation with her I raised the possibility of reporting the abuse to the authorities, but we always encountered the same problem: the evidence she was able to offer was too flimsy for use, and she was unwilling to provide the evidence that was more intimate and would be more specific. This patient had made contact with the police and had told them I was treating her. A police officer did contact me, and I spoke to him about fresh injuries that I could identify by tissue memory. It has to be noted here that the perpetrators of abuse are skilled in either leaving no mark or in making the injury appear to be the outcome of an accident. The client herself provided information that led to the gathering of hard facts, but the evidence was lost—as always seemed to happen—and that was the end of it.

I heard a number of accounts of extreme acts and of occasions when my client had been included in these acts in a manner that caused her to believe she had been helping to kill people. For example, a patient described how, as a child, she had been made to light a pyre on which someone was burned alive, but it was in fact clear from her description of the event that it was not actually her match that lit the pyre. The person telling her to do this had contrived the situation to make her feel guilty for the death of someone that she loved. In this way the abusers establish an ever-increasing control over the abused person. I have never knowingly encountered an abuser personality within the personalities of any patient with DID, just some personalities who are more animal than human: they grunted rather than using words and stuffed food into their mouths, even when the main personality was anorexic.

Conclusion

In this kind of treatment it is important that the patient is my guide as to whether he or she wants treatment at a certain level for a certain aspect of his or her condition. Even if palpation tells me that more treatment is needed, I wait for permission from the patient to go ahead because I need to know that the patient is ready. This is generally true in osteopathy, but especially true of patients with DID. In examination, there may be a wide range of things that call loudly to the treating clinician for attention. Yet these things would take the patient back to experiences or injuries that he or she does not want to know about or does not want you to know about.

Acknowledging pain, as well as experiencing pain, may trigger body memories in the client that awaken associations of psychological trauma with physical trauma and may send the client into apparently unrelated or disproportionate levels of suffering and withdrawal.

My treatment of clients with DID has been more effective when I am able to maintain contact with one personality throughout the session, preferably one that is capable of managing the demands of his or her life in an effective manner. There has been no single approach to treatment, and the need for flexibility and creative thinking is always to the fore.

It is important to remember that these people have been programmed not to respond to therapy. This can be discouraging, and you have to use ingenuity to find ways to get around this barrier. My experience with patients with DID has shown me that they require more than the usual amount of forgiveness, forbearance, and willingness to assume that their intentions are good when the evidence for this is poor; genuine concern for the welfare of the patient has to be given precedence over my own convenience. These qualities might be expressed towards any patient, but patients with DID draw upon them more than most because of the factors that inevitably interfere with their normal life-management skills—for example, resulting in occasional failure to attend appointments. Some of these patients draw from the practitioner a commitment to extend care beyond conventional ranges, crossing the usual boundaries of professional care and relationship into the realm of exercising moral and social responsibility.

At the present state of experience, I would hesitate to claim any permanent pain relief in treating patients with DID, only temporary improvements. In this respect it should be thought of as similar to treating a chronic illness. A feature of DID is that whatever abuse the patient has suffered—whether physical or psychological—the DID is a powerful factor in maintaining the patient's condition of physical pain. The treatment therefore needs to be much more intensive than is usual if there is to be a permanent change. Despite this, treatment is a useful support for these patients because relief from distress has an important value in itself. I believe that achieving even temporary pain relief in a patient with DID is an end worth pursuing. Progressive identification of the various aspects of this condition suggests that the disentangling of some of the threads of pain aetiology, together with the prospect of a measure of enduring relief, is tantalizingly close. Perhaps it could be brought closer by more effective integration of physical and psychological therapy.

CHAPTER THIRTEEN

Opening Pandora's box

Sue Cook

In Greek mythology there is a famous tale about a woman, Pandora, who was entrusted with a special box and the safe keeping of its contents by the god Zeus. She had no idea that inside was every imaginable evil and sorrow that could afflict mankind. She was simply told never to open the lid. She forgot about this box for many years, until one day, coming across it, innocent curiosity overcame her and she lifted the lid, releasing its deadly contents throughout the world. When she realized what was happening, she slammed the lid shut, trapping at the bottom of the box the very thing that could save mankind from endless torment and despair. The world remained an extremely bleak place until one day Pandora chanced to revisit the box again, and, lifting the lid a second time, the box's remaining occupant—hope—flew out in the form of a dove, thus making life in the world worthwhile and bearable even in the face of horror and tragedy.

For adults living with dissociative identity disorder, lifting the lid of their box (also something that in their minds is "not allowed") and uncovering and releasing a host of horrors can be equally devastating. As with Pandora's box, hope is often the last—but the saving—grace to emerge. Once these horrors and their effects have surfaced, they can never be pushed back inside—and, indeed, one would not want them to remain hidden, as they need to be worked with and resolved. Even with hope this is an incredibly difficult and bewildering process, not only for the individual with DID but also for the therapist, support workers, friends, and family who accompany the sufferer on his or her courageous journey to recovery.

My meeting with such a Pandora's box happened seven years ago in the context of my local Anglican church where both myself and Laura, who became my first DID client, worshipped. I had been practising as a therapist for only a year when one Sunday evening my supervisor, who was also a member of this church and knew Laura better than most, asked me if I would pray with her. I remember that it was a communion service and that Laura had been unable to take communion and was sitting in her seat very emotionally distressed. It was only later that I came to understand how triggering communion is for Laura and why. Back then, none of her friends and supporters knew much about the associations with cult rituals and sacraments, and I was probably the most ignorant of all. My supervisor spoke with Laura and accompanied her to the prayer area where, after a while, she left her with me. Laura knew who I was because we had had a few brief conversations in the past year, but nothing more than that. I knew that Laura was what I would call now a vulnerable adult, with an extremely abusive background, but I had no idea then as to the complexity and chronic nature of her trauma. That night she literally fell into my arms and clung to me, sobbing, unable to speak. It totally took me by surprise, as I had been told that Laura found any kind of touch very difficult. As I held her it felt as if I was holding a desperately distraught young child who just needed containment and sanctuary in that moment, so that is what I gave her. She said nothing over the next 20 minutes, and nor did I. I simply stroked her hair and soothed her, until gradually she calmed and settled. I was praying quietly, asking for wisdom for myself and for God to meet with this small abandoned child in the body of a 33-year-old woman and to throw her a lifeline. As it turned out, that lifeline was me! I was the answer to that prayer. I spoke with my supervisor after that evening, suggesting that

Laura should have some counselling. When that was put to Laura, she agreed, with the proviso that she could work with me.

In those first months of working with Laura I was experiencing the full shock and rawness of being faced with a constant stream of horrific material that neither my relatively sheltered life nor training to date had even begun to prepare me for. Hindsight is a wonderful thing, but it did not help me then. Going back to my early notes, where I used to write all my reflections and observations, I find that phrases like "I feel like a witness to a serious traffic accident", "I am battered and totally disorientated", and "I'm not sure I can listen to much more of this stuff" were typical comments in my weekly summations. Interestingly, I would say that I can still feel like that now on a regular basis, except that now I can process my own secondary traumatization much quicker than I could then. Maybe some things never change in terms of our capacity to be impacted by the horrors of our DID clients' Pandora's boxes, whether we are a novice or veteran.

Laura and I started to have a 1½-hour session every Thursday afternoon. We still meet at the same time, on the same day, seven years later. In my mind I would not think of doing anything else on a Thursday afternoon unless I am ill or on holiday. At first I had no real idea how long we might work together, but I knew it would not be just a matter of months and that I was in for the long haul, whatever that meant. What I did not realize was how utterly seriously Laura took my rather glib and idealistic promise early on that I would stay with her for as long as it took. I had no real sense then, as I do now, that that kind of commitment meant limitations and costs to me in terms of my own personal choices and that of my family in order to honour that weekly commitment, which for Laura was set in stone.

In the initial sessions Laura was constantly checking, "Do you believe me, or do you think I am making it up, like the others? They said it was all in my head. The psychiatrist, she said the past wasn't important and I didn't need to keep talking about it, that it made me ill and that I need to focus on now and getting better. She did all the talking. Can I really tell you anything?" I was anxious to be experienced by Laura as a good therapist who was trustworthy and respectful and who allowed her to choose what she needed from therapy rather than being told. I encouraged her to talk and to tell her story exactly as she needed to. I promised her that I would not close her down or have subjects she could not speak about in the sessions, and I assured her that, of course, I would believe everything she told me as being her experience. In my naivety, I did not realize at the time what I was offering, what floodgates I was encouraging her to open, and what the impact would be for us both. I had listened to stories of trauma and abuse with other clients, but never of such severity and such a constancy. There was never any time for me to recover before the next horrific disclosure, which, of course, paralleled Laura's own experience of her trauma.

Each week I met with this friendly, homely, almost cheeky-looking woman in her early thirties who was talkative, intelligent, and highly artistic. She did not work and, in fact, has not been able to hold down a job since her early twenties. She was also very compliant, desperate to please, and very anxious not to upset me. Frequently seeking reassurance, she would ask, "Have I done something wrong?" or "Are you angry with me?" In those early days I used to find the endless repetition of those two questions irritating and wearying, as my assurances never seemed to satisfy Laura for long. Over the years, however, my understanding of the need for absolute obedience and the fear of punishment in a ritual context make Laura's constant checking very understandable.

Laura told me that her family came from Wales and London. What has come out years later through the disclosures of other personalities is that their origins are in Eastern Europe and from a mixed background of Judaism and Christianity, and that they have been involved in satanism for many generations. At the onset of therapy, Laura told me that she was the eldest daughter and, as such, was considered to "belong to Satan" and to exist solely for ritual purposes. Laura said that her mother singled her out for particularly sadistic treatment from birth to the age of 15, when she was forced to leave home three days after giving birth to a baby, who was taken from her. She lived on the streets in London for the next two years. During her first 15 years there had been chronic neglect, brutal cruelty, and emotional deprivation. She was rarely in school, suffered bad health, and had no friends.

These revelations alone shocked me to the core and set off alarm bells inside me concerning what I was getting involved with. As a committed Christian, I have no problem accepting the existence of evil as real and the existence of Satan who has power to destroy and instigate all manner of trauma, hate, and depravity. I knew that I could not underestimate the spiritual assaults and oppression that I might be subject to when dealing with a client who had grown up in such an evil environment. I had to consider whether I could handle such a challenge and what I was going to put in place to prevent myself from being overwhelmed. Prayer was then, and still is, a great resource for me, giving me strength, comfort, perseverance, peace, and even courage, because I often felt very daunted by the task I faced in the early months and the years that have followed. Laura, too, has a very strong Christian faith, and the ability to relate to each other on that level has facilitated trust and attunement.

Each week in those early months Laura would come with a new story of horrific abuse, neglect, and cruelty involving parents, siblings, doctors, and animals. In one session she told me about being stripped naked by her mother, tied up, and left in the attic for several days, aged 3 or 4, with only her own urine to drink, as a punishment for wetting her knickers. Another time she told me about being chained up in the garden shed, again younger than 5 years old, with several large dogs who had sex with her. She was then left for hours afterwards and made to eat dog food and bark like a dog until she believed that is what she was. On another occasion, she told me about going into hospital to have her tonsils out when she was 8 years old. Far from it being the traumatic experience that it can be for a lot of children of that age, it was a haven for her where people spoke gently to her, took care of her, and gave her ice cream to eat. None of her family visited, and no one hurt her for six whole days. When the day came for her to be discharged, Laura remembers begging the nurses and doctors not to send her home because "her Mummy hurt her". She told me that the staff just laughed at her and dismissed her protestations, saying that they had met her mother and she was lovely. So Laura returned back to her life of daily and nightly abuse and terror, where there was no protection or respite.

Every session would bring up a new story like these, which would leave me feeling shell-shocked, angry, and helpless, with a myriad questions spinning around in my head. How could anyone treat a child in such a way? Why did neighbours, teachers, nurses—anyone—not notice something was amiss and report it? How come when Laura did manage to speak up and ask for help, no one listened and no one checked her story? How could these sorts of things happen in the midst of a civilized society and escape notice? What Laura and I only discovered years later—from her other personalities—was that neighbours were involved in the ritual group, as were teachers at her school and the family doctor, so that those whom Laura thought as a child might offer her safety were perpetrators too.

Being able to contain the horror and shock of what Laura was describing without appearing to be repulsed, sickened, and overwhelmed by it—when, in fact, I was all those things—was very stressful and draining. I experienced a degree of contamination and violation just listening to these things. Laura told me that she would leave my house after a session and often by the time she had reached the end of my road she would be shaking or be sick. What I did not tell her was that my response was not much different! Many times after she left I would sit on my sofa and cry. I would wander around the house distracted and unable to settle to any task. Often I would phone my supervisor and, without going through the details, because that increased my distress, I would tell her about my feelings of horror and helplessness and ask her to pray with me, which she readily did. Prayer really helped me to separate myself from what I had just experienced, to "de-slime" and to instil hope again for the efficacy of therapy, because a lot of the time it did not have the effect of making either of us feel very good. I never knew how I would be after a session with Laura, so I made her my last appointment of the day in order to give me sufficient recovery time if I needed it. Nowadays I can have a 30-minute break, a cup of tea, and continue with other clients because experience has taught me how to dissociate sufficiently from the material, which is an absolute necessity for anyone who is going to do this work on a day-to-day basis. Seven years ago I did not know how to do this.

In subsequent years, I spent hundreds of hours listening to accounts of chronic and enduring abuse. Often I would think I could never hear anything more shocking and sickening than what Laura disclosed in our current session, and then the following week she would describe something even worse. So my level of tolerance was continually being stretched. Accounts of torture were followed by being buried alive, followed by cannibalism and child sacrifice, and so it went on. Much of my secondary trauma was due to the extreme forensic nature of the abuse. Every incident was a serious crime that would warrant years of imprisonment. Laura was describing an underworld that was far more depraved and lawless than anything depicted in Dickensian England. The intensity of my exposure was another factor. I was not listening to just hours of details of abuse, as many therapists who work with less traumatized clients do, but hundreds of hours of hard-core criminal acts, which takes its toll.

Within three months, I began to meet a lot of Laura's personalities, mainly traumatized children and young teenagers. Each one held memories, feelings, and beliefs about the abuse that they had been created to take. This enabled Laura to maintain the illusion that any abuse had happened to someone else and not her. Thus, Laura was free to a great extent to focus on the functions of normal everyday living: being a committed Christian, attending church and a Bible study group, attending college and studying for A-Levels, and spending many hours designing and sewing the most intricate and beautiful cross-stitch pictures, for which she has a remarkable talent. At times, it felt more comfortable for me as a therapist to collude with Laura's denial in order to cope with my own inability to neatly file away some of the horrors and almost unbelievable accounts that I was hearing, in order to deal more easily with my increasing dilemma—what do I do with this stuff?

From the beginning of therapy, Laura needed considerable support outside session time. She was—and still is—an extraordinary client compared to others that I worked with at the time, so I was prepared to have more flexible boundaries. With Laura I was dealing with many clients within a client: child and teenage identities who had needs that could not be neatly encompassed in a 90-minute weekly slot. Laura, and the other named identities that were known to us in the first 18 months, would phone, text, and email me frequently in order to be reassured that I was still there and that nothing had happened to me. That took some getting used to, and, if I am honest, it felt a little weird, if not bizarre, at first, to be communicating with babies, children, and teenagers of both sexes, sometimes in the space of one phone call or a single session. It was certainly a steep learning curve, and I often wondered if I was doing the right thing, but it did seem to have a stabilizing effect.

Laura often described herself in those early months as feeling scared and unsafe. I assumed that was because she was experiencing trauma re-enactments, which made it really hard to stay grounded and not "lose time". This left her feeling very confused and disorientated. While this explanation was correct, it was only partially correct. What I did not realize, because Laura herself did not, was that the abuse was not just in the past but was still happening in the present to some of her personalities. Meetings were arranged and journeys were taken back to the family by other personalities who were still loyal to the group and who were, as yet, unknown to Laura. Her sense of danger was thus based on present reality, not just past memories or emotional insecurity with me.

I knew that when Laura "lost time", her personalities could do things and go places that Laura had no memory or knowledge about. When it was buying cream cakes or milkshakes or ordering goods from catalogues, the worst outcome was that she put on weight and got into debt, which was manageable. I had no idea, at this stage, that there were many other adult personalities yet to emerge who were doing far more dangerous things against Laura's will. They were engaging in activities that were criminal and impacting upon her safety, such as taking her to ceremonies at home and abroad—when supposedly on holiday—and being subject to rapes and beatings. All this only came out years later.

I gradually learned that issues of safety were heightened according to dates on the calendar. Halloween and the month leading up to it was one of the worst times for Laura. A year after we had begun to work together, she became increasingly mentally unstable, finding it almost impossible to stay grounded and unable to sleep because of night terrors. I was afraid that she might commit suicide but was reluctant to pursue the route of short-term hospitalization because I feared, based on her past history, that she would be misdiagnosed and thus treated inappropriately. With no other options, I just had to watch constantly, and I finally invited her to spend the night at my home over Halloween. It felt like a drastic step, and beyond my remit, but there were no other helpful options. So I decided to provide the containment and safety that Laura needed in order to sleep and rest. My instinct told me that it was the right thing to do, and I have done it again several times since with no regrets. I stayed with her throughout the night, providing a safe presence, reassurance, and contact when she needed it. Amazingly, she slept for seven hours, which was the first decent sleep she had had for days. The next morning she cried and said that I had done something no one else had ever done: stayed with her when she was scared and not hurt her. She was deeply moved, and so was I. She needed a safe house, and I provided it. Only years later have I realized that I had not just provided emotional safety but physical safety, as she probably would have gone back to a ceremony that night if I had not been minding her.

Seven years into therapy, it would appear, from the revelations of many new personalities that have emerged over the years, that none of Laura's family members are safe. In the first 18 months we did not know this, and subsequently Laura continued to go back to the group to be hurt herself and, under duress, commit criminal acts against others during ceremonies. This awareness has come only years after the events, as personalities who were involved emerged and spoke of their experiences. My ignorance at that time did not serve Laura well. I now know that clients actually get hurt on the dates of important ceremonies, so it is particularly important to anticipate possible danger and put some arrangements in place.

Laura had an idealized view of her siblings, and her strong sense of duty to the family impaired her judgement regarding having contact. She talked about numerous nieces and nephews whom she doted on and did not wish to be cut off from, and, with hindsight, this put her in danger. In the early months, she would protect her family, even the ones she acknowledged as perpetrators, in order to protect others, and especially the children of her siblings. There was never any talk of reporting to the police the catalogue of horrific crimes that she had described to me. The whole process would have been too traumatic for Laura, who had not had any good experiences with the police up to that point. In recent times, however, Laura has begun to liaise with a police unit that is unusually well informed about DID. She and other personalities have had some very positive experiences talking about both past abuse and recent criminal incidents, which are being investigated currently.

In the early days of therapy, as well as Laura's resistance to making her perpetrators known and reporting them, I was not tempted to go to the police myself, for a whole host of reasons. I had no idea how we might explain to the police, who deal only in evidence and provable hard facts, incidents that lacked both these components. I had no way of verifying any of the things that Laura had told me, even though I knew I believed her. She could not prove any of the crimes she spoke about happening in the past, as it was too long ago. More crucially, she was not ready yet to give specific details about people, addresses, and other information that might tie in with accounts given by other ritual abuse survivors and might therefore be useful to the police. I considered that it was highly unlikely that a police officer would believe the accounts of horrific ritual abuse that Laura's personalities had shared with me or would take Laura and her separate identities seriously. I could not envisage that anyone other than a therapist would be prepared to talk with other personalities, as well as with the core person. Would they simply dismiss her as mentally unstable and delusional? What would the police make of me? Would they consider both me and my client to be a little crazy and wasting their time? I did not want to look foolish, especially as I was fairly inexperienced in the whole area of DID. I was very unsure of myself and what I was doing, which made me very reluctant to talk with anyone who was likely to cross-examine me. This changed once a formal diagnosis of DID was secured for Laura, together with funding for additional treatment at the Clinic for Dissociative Studies in London three years ago. But, back in the early days, both Laura and I felt too vulnerable and often in denial. She and her personalities could hardly bear to tell me—someone whom she was coming to trust—about these criminal acts, let alone strangers whom she would perceive as suspicious and unbelieving, at best, and hostile at worst. In any case, they represented power and authority, which is a frightening and formidable combination for any survivor of ritual abuse.

In the relationship with me, Laura's greatest fear has always been that I would one day see her as a murderess and perpetrator, who was no better than the other members of her family. She was terrified that I would abandon her and turn her over to the police to face what she deserved—namely, imprisonment. Laura has indeed committed some very serious crimes against others, including murder. But I saw Laura more as a victim than a perpetrator of crime, even as she gradually began to tell me not just about crimes committed against her, but crimes that she as a child and teenager had been forced to do to others. Back then, as now, there was no one else to corroborate any of her accounts and no witnesses—apart from internal ones—which meant I felt I could do nothing other than sit with these awful revelations for the time being. One thing I am utterly convinced about, and always have been, is that Laura's participation in the past was never willingly entered into. She and her personalities were always under extreme duress, rather like having a gun held to your head, so there was no real choice. She was always terrified and driven by the inner compulsion of her personalities to do exactly as told and not to think about it. Now, as an adult, she is still triggered at times into those deeply traumatized parts who hold the memories, feelings, and beliefs of the past and still are conditioned to engage in ritual activity. It is a bit like being hypnotized to go and do something totally out of character with your normal self, with no power to resist and no conscious awareness of what you are doing .

My priority at that time was to help Laura face and own these unspeakable traumas as having happened to her and to resolve and integrate them into her experience so that she could get past them, not to try to bring the perpetrators to justice. As I have already said, that was not what Laura wanted anyway, and early on in therapy there seemed nothing to suggest that her nieces and nephews were in any immediate danger. Seven years later, as I hear almost on a weekly basis many new revelations about Laura's family, those children may well be at risk, but as I am not in possession of their personal details we cannot make any checks. Laura assures me that they are safe; but how does she know for sure? That question niggles away at me, and I feel quite helplessly in a dilemma, but I cannot force Laura to reveal more than she is able to.

The longer I work with DID, the more I am aware of the complexities of this condition and how each client needs a very individual approach from his or her therapist, and preferably his or her "team", in order to manage well each dilemma and crisis—from which there seems to be no let-up—and contain what is too vast for just one pair of arms to hold. Many times I wonder if I and others have done the right thing in lifting the lid off this box of horrors. The level of suffering and pain continues to be so great, as Laura and other DID clients recover co-consciousness and are no longer largely protected from their history but are having to face it and own it as theirs and integrate it. Making sense of it all is not something to even attempt in the beginning. For them, and for us, that comes much later. Staying with the not-knowing is a wonderful concept that has helped me persevere when it felt easier to give up. Seven years on, I still find it hard at times to keep going in this work. Even when I close my office door, these amazing survivors stay in my thoughts and disturb my sleep with the compelling, and at times seemingly impossible, task of bringing the torture to an end and enabling them to reach a place of safety at last.

CHAPTER FOURTEEN

From social conditioning to mind control

Valerie Sinason

"Man does not have the right to develop his own mind.
This kind of liberal orientation has great appeal. We must
electrically control the brain. Some day armies and generals
will be controlled by electric stimulation of the brain."

Jose Delgado, *Congressional Record*, No. 262E, Vol. 118, 1974

"Ordinary people, simply doing their jobs, and without
any particular hostility on their part, can become agents
in a terrible destructive process. Moreover, even when the
destructive effects of their work become patently clear,
and they are asked to carry out actions incompatible with
fundamental standards of morality, relatively few people have
the resources needed to resist authority."

Stanley Milgram (1974)

T he year was 1992. The former military American man was
lying on the London hospital bed in a state of terror. He
did not know why he had flown to England when he had
no friends or family here, but he knew he had to kill someone.

After an unbearable period in which he had become aware of the charged meaning of a word, "delta", which meant something extremely dangerous to him, he had gone to his local GP. The GP had anxiously referred him to a psychiatrist. The psychiatrist had been sympathetic but thought the man was a paranoid schizophrenic and sectioned him.

He had spent several months in hospital trying to find someone who would understand the nature of his terror and feeling increasingly suicidal and despairing. Finally, just before he was in danger of a lengthy section, a new senior registrar had joined the staff who thought she might be aware of the nature of his problems. She had persuaded the psychiatrist to allow an assessment from a colleague, Dr Margot, who was experienced with this kind of presenting problem.

Dr Margot had rung the Tavistock Clinic to invite myself and Dr Robert Hale (a former Director of the Portman Clinic and a consultant forensic psychiatrist and psychoanalyst) as independent observers to the assessment, as she considered it was of a nature that required shared thinking and witnessing. She had asked the senior registrar to discuss with the patient whether he would allow such witnesses, and he had agreed.

In the event, Dr Hale was not free and I went alone. I felt very nervous. Dr Hale and I had been given the background information above, but nothing further. We had been working with children and adults who came with disclosures of ritual abuse, and some of these had also had different degrees of dissociation. However, I had not encountered any clinical presentation like this.

As we entered the single room off the main ward, Lieutenant Romola (not his real name) raised himself wearily on the bed. The senior registrar introduced us and then left us. Romola was a muscular man with olive skin and a shock of dark hair and terrified eyes with large dark circles round them. He looked as if he had not slept for days. He stared at my colleague, Dr Margot. She did not move or blink under the intensity of his scan.

"You know, don't you," he said with a strong clear American accent.

"Something," she said. "Where have you got to?"

He waved at the hospital side room deprecatingly. "This is where I go for telling the truth. In England. Not Russia, not America, England."

"Yep. That's how it is," said Dr Margot.

"I need the delta de-activated, or I am a vegetable here for life."

"Know who it's aimed at?"

"No."

"No wonder you needed help. You're a life-saver," Dr Margot replied.

"Thank you."

I was as surprised by Dr Margot's language as by the man's and had no idea what they were talking about.

"How did you find out about the delta?"

His face suddenly changed, and a metallic robotic sound came from his mouth. "This is Level 33. You should not be here. Unauthorized personnel. Everyone on this level will be wiped out in ten seconds if you do not give the correct password."

I looked in terror at Dr Margot, who remained calm. Romola's heart rate was speeding up, and his face was turning blue.

"I need Level 33 password now. I order you," barked Margot, suddenly, like a colonel.

A shy, low voice came out of Romola's mouth and provided the password, a number, and Margot repeated it with great authority.

Romola relaxed, and the blue colour started moving from his face. Another sound came from his lips, which sounded like lift doors closing and opening.

This procedure continued with a stop at different "levels" until we reached the ground.

Suddenly another sound came from Romola's mouth. This sounded like the voice on a telephone-answering machine. The voice gave out telephone numbers, which Dr Margot wrote down. Then came a man's name, which I had not heard before. There was no affect in the expression of the voice.

Then everything was silent again.

Romola's face changed dramatically. A new beatific expression came over him. He looked at us and said, "Thank you for coming. I can take over from here. You may watch. I have deleted the name. That man is now safe. He will not be killed."

There was silence.

"What a beautiful garden," he said, "everything is green here." Suddenly the smile left his face. "You, here. I should have known it was you, Dr Green. I do not have to obey you any more."

His face shut down, blank like a computer screen.

After what felt like an eternity, but was probably ten or fifteen minutes, Romola stretched his arms and legs and sat up. He looked at us, stunned. "I feel like a new man," he said. "What happened?" He looked at Dr Margot and her pad with the phone numbers. "You did it. You have taken it out."

That experience has never left me. I have never seen anything like that before or since, and any dramatic changes I have witnessed have rarely come from a single meeting. What do we make of such an encounter? Could it be a mixture of fact and fiction, a post-traumatic reworking of a war experience? How did this man get into such a psychic condition? If it was psychosis, surely it could not be answered by Dr Margot's response? And if it was true, if the advent of computers and military technology could join together to commit a mind-control crime, what are the chances of a health service professional recognizing it or being trained to work with it? What are the chances of any such crime even getting to the police?

In the years since this encounter, I have worked in a highly specialized way with children and adults, with or without a learning disability, who have experienced ritual abuse. Some have a dissociative disorder. None have had a military role like Lieutenant Romola, but a small number have recounted experiences with a military aspect linked to a military base. And in this time I have come to understand something further, whether true or not, about the significance of a Dr Green.

Experiments in obedience

Romola's moment of freedom was underlined by the sentence, "I do not have to obey you any more." Obedience is the basis of most socializations—the family, school, religion, and work—and, of course, is even more crucial within the armed services. For this forensic book, it is worth thinking about how many crimes committed by unwilling perpetrators have been committed under the name of obedience. To understand the crucial role of obedience, we need to look at the work of Stanley Milgram (1963, 1974; see also Blass, 2002, 2004).

Stanley Milgram was born into a Jewish family in New York in 1933. He studied political science as a first degree and then took a PhD in psychology. While at Yale and still in his late twenties, he conducted some memorable experiments that have been replicated many times over and have a significant and painful place in our understanding of human behaviour (Milgram, 1963, 1974).

With the trial of Adolf Eichmann causing enormous international publicity and the rethinking of Nazi war crimes, Milgram was influenced by the ground-breaking work of New York philosopher and fellow Jewish immigrant Hannah Arendt (1963), who wrote that Eichmann was not a sadist but a bureaucrat. This chimed with Milgram's concerns around obeying orders and the ethical, moral, and philosophical issues involved. He devised an experiment that tested whether people would obey an order that went contrary to their views on the importance of human dignity and care if a "researcher" told them to.

In the first experiments in 1961, he found that 65% of the participants were willing to administer to another person a 450-volt shock—which they thought was real but was not, and the "victim/learner" was an actor—although many were uncomfortable doing so. However, even those who were uncomfortable, or did not give a shock beyond 300 volts, did not demand the banning of the experiment.

There was willingness in international audiences at that time, as a result of Milgram's work, to examine what "obeying orders" meant. This was easiest when looked at retrospectively at Nazi atrocities, despite the equally strong emotional need to see Nazi behaviour as "inhuman". However, there was little social capacity for taking the same concept forwards. The behaviour of the US army in Guantanamo Bay and in Abu Ghraib, the current concern in America with "rank abuse" (sexual abuse of female military personnel by those in higher ranks), the speed of the Rwandan genocide, Bosnia, "honour killings" in the United Kingdom (let alone elsewhere)—all these point to the centrality of obedience in the social and religious psyche. Lloyd deMause (1974) is one of the few psychoanalytic historians to endorse this, backed by the work of crusading psychoanalysts such as Alice Miller (1980), who points to the long-term consequences of beating, submission, and obedience in childhood. Indeed, what does it mean that the United Kingdom is still one of the countries where child beating is allowed, but comparable assault on adults is illegal?

While many of Milgram's colleagues and psychology students expected only a tiny percent to inflict the electric shocks, the 65% figure has been replicated in other experiments and highlights a social danger and dynamic that individual therapists need to be aware of. In what ways do clients (or, indeed, junior police officers, psychiatrists, lawyers in the workplace, or students on a course) comply in order to be "obedient" and pleasing? How does the power differential impact on treatment?

However, while there might be individual members of any profession who exploit the power differential, what are the individual and social dangers involved when, outside the crucible of a single experiment, junior men and women are pressured to take part in ongoing activities that hurt others for the supposed sake of a political ideal, a God, or a country? Indeed, there is a non-sexual equivalent of the Hollywood casting couch in almost every human arena. Obeying orders is no longer sanctioned as an excuse for atrocities and torture, yet obeying orders is a strong social instinct.

Second World War and post-Second World War mind control

With obedience, shame, and fear of exclusion all being basic instincts, what happens when political and financial support is given to those who utilize such knowledge abusively? Every period of human history provides examples, and these abusive cultures and practices are transmitted through generational transmission.

The ritual abuse practices that I have spent the last 17 years working with appear to be hangovers from medieval Christian religious practices of intolerance, torture, and execution. Terror of hellfire and Satan acted as a form of social control in troubled times to traumatize people and was passed down while those with a secure attachment to their religion and country did not require Gods of hate. This makes ritual abuse survivors an anomalous minority. For some, the abuse is embedded in a modern mind-control program, carried out within a political belief system, with technology taking the place of biblical imagery. For others, there is a complex experience of a belief system embedded in the mind control.

These combinations found a disturbing home in the international upheaval and trauma of the Second World War. Operation Paperclip (Keith, 1997; Marks, 1979; Ross, 2006) welcomed a large number of Germans brought up in the Nazi belief system because they were prepared to continue using and developing Nazi techniques for social control. Scientists, psychiatrists, and mind-control experimenters were offered new identities and brought to America with cooperation between the US State Department, army intelligence, and the structures that became the Central Intelligence Agency. This toxic immigration was to have devastating consequences that are still reverberating. Japanese scientists who had performed human medical experiments were treated in the same way. They were offered immunity from prosecution in exchange for data on biological warfare research.

In order to imagine now the mindset of politicians facing annihilation fears, we can look at the American response to the traumatic destruction of the Twin Towers (a war, thousands of deaths, extraordinary rendition, and torture) to understand more fully what could happen if a whole country was at risk. The longing that led to research for a Manchurian Candidate—a programmed human who could be sent out to pick up enemy secrets and return with them without being noticed (Marks, 1979)—is entirely credible, and is proven by Congressional records, in the context of that time.

It is not surprising that such fears and wishes found a way into political action and links with Nazi former enemies. Heinrich Himmler and Josef Mengele had been involved in eugenic and other forms of experimentation that were to lay the seeds of some aspects of programmed DID. While Great Britain, as a Second World War victor, had a chance to mock Himmler's *Lebersborn* project, aimed to create an Aryan super-race, the seriousness of the venture has been minimized. The occult aspects of Hitler's belief system has, in the United Kingdom, often been trivialized in occult jewellery items rather than mainstream discussion. Mengele's scientific experiments at Auschwitz, and others at Dachau, allowed brainwashing experiments to be attempted that involved the use of drugs as well as electric shocks, other torture, and criminally created DID. Mengele was also known as "Dr Green". The psychologist Corydon Hammond (1992) has risked major discreditation—but has also received gratitude—for speaking about these issues. Where do we put the testimony of survivors, such as Lieutenant Romola, who testify to a Dr Green, a Nazi?

Operation BLUEBIRD was approved by CIA director Allen Dulles in 1950 and renamed Operation ARTICHOKE in 1951. Research by Colin Ross (2006) shows that the creation of dissociative identities was fully endorsed. As well as being potential couriers and spies, the subjects could function, in effect, as the human equivalent of a tape recorder, a computer, or camera and be amnesic for the entire episode. The memorized material could then be retrieved by a programmer using a previously implanted code or signal.

Operation ARTICHOKE involved the development of special, extreme methods of interrogation. Officials responsible for the ARTICHOKE program were very concerned with the problem of disposing of "blown agents" and with the task of finding a way to produce amnesia in operatives who had seen too much and could no longer be relied upon.

In 1953, the CIA initiated Project MKULTRA. This was a decade-long research programme designed to produce and test drugs and biological agents that could be used for mind control and behaviour modification. Major hospitals and research centres took part in 149 subprojects (Bowart, 1977; Keith, 1997). LSD and other drugs were used on unwitting subjects to check behaviour alterations. Drugs, combined with electric shocks, were used on subjects who would not be able to complain—such as psychiatric patients and prisoners, especially black ones (Keith, 1997). How do we deal with a topic that, even to those of us who are used to working with ritual abuse, sounds so bizarre? And how can the perpetrators of such acts be brought to justice? While mafia or black-market or gang behaviour can have a significant impact on a geographical area, a national area, and the national psyche, this umbrella of projects involved a large section of intellectual, cultural, and scientific life in a major Western country.

The quarter-century transmission

In the same way that many survivors are only able to disclose abuse from early childhood in their middle to late twenties, when they are free of the parental home and authority, many unethical acts at a national level are only revealed twenty to twenty-five years later. The 1970s saw a remarkable number of factual, rigorously researched exposés. Since 1975 the freedom of information requests in the United States have led to many documents being released by the CIA.

Project MKULTRA was publicly exposed through lawsuits filed by Canadian survivors and their families. The CIA and Canadian government settled out of court so as not to be required to officially admit to any wrongdoing. Dr Ewen Cameron, a leading psychiatrist, had developed techniques used by Nazi scientists to wipe out the existing personalities of people in his care. Cameron received CIA research money, and, in addition to electroshock, drug injections, and lobotomies, he conceived the technique of "psychic driving", wherein unsuspecting patients were kept in a drug-induced coma for several weeks and administered a regimen of electroshocks, while helmets were strapped to their heads and repetitive auditory messages were transmitted at variable speeds (Cameron, 1956; Ross, 2006; Thomas, 1989). Many of those exploited were abused orphanage children.

Not every scientist involved in such crimes remained silent. Dr George Estabrooks was key in creating hypnotically induced dissociation. A Rhodes scholar with a doctorate from Harvard, he has written extensively on hypnosis, but he also chose in the 1970s to become more explicit (Estabrooks, 1971). As we know in the field of trauma, some things are so unbearable to consider that, even when stated explicitly, they evoke little discussion. He spoke of how the hypnotic courier was a brilliant invention and described how he hypnotized an Army captain to respond to hypnotic suggestions and be amnesic to it. He said, "The system is virtually foolproof. As exemplified by this case, the information was 'locked' in Smith's unconscious for retrieval by the only two people who knew the combination. The subject had no conscious memory of what happened, so could not spill the beans." Estabrooks commented on how relatively easy that was compared to work in the 1920s, "where clinical hypnotists had learned how to split certain complex individuals into multiple personalities". However, Estabrooks claimed he did this with another subject, a vulnerable Marine lieutenant, whom he split into a main personality who was a serious communist and a second personality who was a loyal American and would report back. He claimed that the enemy suspected this trick and "played the same trick on us later" (Estabrooks, 1971).

While some practitioners remained secret, Jose Delgado, Professor of Physiology at Yale University, was content to make clear his views on human rights:

> The possibility of scientific annihilation of personal identity, or even worse, its purposeful control, has sometimes been considered a future threat more awful than atomic holocaust. Even physicians have expressed doubts about the propriety of physical tampering with the psyche, maintaining that personal identity should be inviolable, that any attempt to modify individual behaviour is unethical. . . . These objections, however, are debatable. [Delgado, 1971, p. 214]

Are we witnessing a development from child abuse that is justified by archaic and medieval religion into technology-based abuse of adults who have been "softened up" by institutional or family abuse in which there is a belief that, at times of war, "freedom" is worth fighting for using tools that can only belong to those championing unfreedom?

When crime wears a white coat and has many degrees, it is much harder for justice to be accessed.

From social conditioning to mind control

Mind-control processes and programs are extensions, of course, of ordinary social and familial conditioning of children. We are usually born into a certain kind of family, or social class, or religious background that creates a template that is powerful but often invisible to us.

For example, at one extreme we have the child victims of cruel social and religious beliefs who never feel free. Jonathan at the age of 8 years was terrorized by the village priest whose Old Testament X-rated Hell and God of cruelty bore no resemblance to the God of love he found in his adult life. Nevertheless, in the small hours of night he lay awake still terrified as a man of 38 by the sadistic priest's vision and a feeling he should obey it. He was mind-controlled, although such a description is rarely given to "normative" socialization processes. We can think here of the famous, allegedly Jesuit, saying: "Give me a child to the age of 7 and you can have him for the rest of his life." As soon as suicide bombers appeared in the last decade, there was an equal concern about the mind-controlling aspects of some distortions of Islam.

On the everyday part of the continuum, we have Mary, aged 41 years, brought up in a poor but loving home, who after a promotion at work bought herself a new dress instead of buying a second-hand one as her poor parents used to do. Although her parents were long dead and she was extremely well paid, she always felt bad at carrying out such an "extravagant" act. At one level, we are all mind controlled through ordinary familial and cultural transmission.

However, the term "mind control" is a more explicit extension of that process in which something is deliberately instilled in a victim with the aim of creating an obedient slave. The desire to have a Manchurian Candidate—a living robot or slave—has been around since the start of history, as has slavery. Do we have to engage with it? Unfortunately, those of us dealing with clients presenting with such narratives, or partial narratives, have to.

Research and writing on mind control seems to follow two very different trajectories. In the first, the history of military and government mind-control programs in the West from the Second World War to the present has the benefit of the declassification of government documents, as well as the words and testimonies of survivors and their families and supporters (e.g. Ross, 2000, 2006; Starrs, 2005). This also includes topics that I have not mentioned in detail, such as electronic harassment and brain electrode implants (Ross, 2006).

The second trajectory follows qualitative accounts by survivors and their families, and those working with them, who have initially come with ritual abuse narratives and dissociative disorders. There are, of course, no official documents for this. Very few people—let alone psychoanalytic psychotherapists (C. Smith, 2003)—work with both these strands to understand how this toxic transmission takes place or how to learn from the clinical and ethical lessons. The international research by Becker and colleagues (chapter 3) is rare in showing the significant link being caused by the recruitment of cult and other victims into formal mind-control programs.

Mind control and dissociative identity disorder as a symptom of criminal intent

What, then, happens when a child or adult who has presented with what we considered was attachment-based DID—usually evidence in itself of serious crimes against them—starts speaking of mind control? How do we respond when we are informed by alter after alter that the multiplicity of the system has been deliberately created by a group (which may or may not include some family members)? Considering deliberate creation of multiple personality states means facing up to something hard to comprehend.

Dissociation as a creative defence against relational trauma is appalling enough to consider, thinking of an overwhelmed small child dealing with impossible burdens. However, to consider the deliberate creation of a fragmented mind enters another sphere of intentionality with links stretching back to Auschwitz and then back further to earliest history.

Indeed, David Icke (2002), who deals with a variety of both verified and unverified mind-control issues, focuses on Mengele's realization that torture and making someone watch torture could shatter "a person's mind into a honeycomb of self-contained compartments or amnesic barriers" (p. 282). Colin Ross (2006), in his rigorously researched study of CIA papers, shows that the Manchurian Candidate is fact and not fiction, and he describes the experiments conducted by psychiatrists to create amnesia, new identities, hypnotic access codes, and new memories in the minds of experimental subjects. How can we hope for police investigations when it is an actual government-sponsored agency that has committed the crime? What are the links to British equivalent crimes? Indeed, some of the survivors who showed evidence of mind-control procedures lived on or near military bases.

Other supposed mind programs: fictitious, true, or a mixture?

This section is very much a work in progress. It is an attempt to share some of the narratives I have heard from colleagues, clients, and individuals from around the world.

It is hard enough for justice to be done with the crimes inflicted in earliest childhood that cause most dissociation we have worked with, but crimes inflicted on survivors of early familial, intrafamilial, or extrafamilial abuse by military and other organizations with the aid of modern technology (including electronic implants) are not even named as offences. Some narratives, or aspects of narratives, we hear, are linked to possible belief systems in secret societies. These may or may not be true, but the survivors certainly believe in and have internalized what they have been told. This is true of all forms of abuse. The genuine victims coming forward to speak of these programs highlight the fact that evidence of a crime is in the victim. However, finding out the exact nature of the crime can be very hard when there is also inbuilt betrayal, misinformation, and deception as part of the system. Translating this into accessing justice and forensic analysis here is even harder. Where deliberately created DID moves beyond government and the military to religious or alleged religious belief systems, people find it even harder to get to a first base in the justice system. Given that only 2% of abuse cases get to court, and only 4% of perpetrators are convicted, we can see what an extra problem mind control causes.

Monarch programming

"Monarch" is said to be a subsection of the ARTICHOKE and MKULTRA programs. However, as Keith (1997) comments, it has received more argument and publicity than the other programs. While practitioners have spoken of their patients who have suffered through Monarch (Hammond, 1992), and some victims and their supporters have come forward to write about it (Phillips & O'Brien, 1995), there is—unlike military mind control—no equivalent of declassified materials. Indeed, as Colin Ross (private communication, 2008) has said, "I've heard about Monarch from many people going back to 1992. I filed Freedom of Information requests concerning Monarch with the CIA, DIA, and each branch of the US military, but got back only a statement that they had no information on it. Monarch could be a real program or an urban legend or a cover name for programs that actually have different names." Nevertheless, clients who have spoken to me about Monarch have provided a variety of meanings. Some see the link with the Monarch butterfly, as a description of the cruelty of children restrained with bent, tied legs who are tortured until alters are produced, who see themselves as butterflies; others see it is as representing depersonalization and a sense of looking down from a height at the self being tortured.

Illuminati is a name that refers to several groups—real, a mixture of truth and distortion, and fictitious. Historically, it refers specifically to an Enlightenment secret society founded in 1776 by Adam Weishaupt. Whether people we encounter who say they are Illuminati, or have been hurt by Illuminati programs, are genuine direct descendants from the 1776 group, or from new groups seeking to link themselves to that history, or from those with a fictitious disorder, the point is that whatever the victim believes is what becomes internalized.

Those who speak of links with the Illuminati see the fact that the Monarch butterfly returns to its home as symbolic, and they also point to the occult meanings of butterflies. The Gnostics saw the butterfly as a symbol of corrupt flesh, and *psyche* meant both butterfly and soul.

Out of some people who show signs of Monarch programming, a significant number come from, or believe they come from, satanist or Luciferian bloodlines. It is reported that CIA controllers sometimes dressed up in satanist costumes to further traumatize the children, also providing a cover that would not be believed if the children ever spoke of the abuse. It is again a separate question as to whether the controllers were, in fact, using such names for the purpose of further hurting children and adults.

I need to state here, as I have before (Sinason, 1994), that I am in no way saying satanism is equated with crime. Indeed, some satanists I have met are victims of disturbed sadistic clerics who have so threatened them with Hellfire that they have joined the other side as a defence against torture. There are satanists who would hurt no one—and some priests, vicars, rabbis, and mullahs who have.

Within Monarch, several levels of programming can be accessed through Greek letters to gain the alter with the function that is required. The Greek letters that colleagues and I have heard are alpha, beta, gamma, delta (which was named by Romola), and omega (which is a "self-destruct" form of programming also known as "Code Green")

I do not know how such ideas have spread and how many groups have borrowed the idea and technology from elsewhere, like a cook trying different recipes, or how much it comes from a shared experimental interest, power game, or belief system. Nevertheless, the crime of creating alters deliberately in this way is something we have seen, and the proof of this is within the DID.

Stages of torture as described by people who have come to us

The initial stage in the deliberate creation of dissociation, according to those who come to us, as well as in the extensive literature, begins *in utero*. The pregnant woman is hurt in order to induce dissociation in the foetus pre-birth. This is primarily achieved through the use of electric shocks. Sexual abuse begins after birth, as well as sensory deprivation after a short period of "bonding". As the baby grows and becomes verbal, there is hypnotism, double-bind coercion, pleasure–pain reversals, food, water, sleep and sensory deprivation, along with various drugs and the programs to create the new alters.

The next stage is to ensure specific alters can keep code numbers and messages. Lights, sounds, colours, electric shocks, computers, and virtual reality are all used here. Programming is updated periodically and reinforced through visual, auditory, and written mediums. Many therapists get a shock when a DID client shows up after an erasing "top-up" in which all recently acquired information has been erased.

As the child grows, popular and loved universal children's entertainment is abused in order to keep up the social conditioning. For example, major children's films from the *Wizard of Oz* to *Alice in Wonderland* are used. Many of the recent Disney movies and cartoons are used in a twofold manner. By being enjoyable and mainstream, it adds to a discrediting process when children speak of abusive triggers involving loved cartoon figures, as well as adding to the indoctrination of Monarch children.

Sometimes alters are named after colours, gemstones, or planets and do not experience these as names only. They perceive themselves, and have been constructed to see themselves, as these entities as part of a program.

We know that survivors of some extreme abuse are easily hypnotizable as well, and some could be repeating specially fed disinformation.

Unanswered questions

The themes above seem to apply to people with DID who are mind-controlled, and many of them apply to ritual abuse victims who are not dissociative. My own experience of long-term work with those disclosing a narrative of mind control or military mind control is small. However, as a result of the highly specialized group of areas I work in, people have come to me to report aspects of programs that have been noted in Monarch or MKULTRA. Does this mean they are part of a military programme or that other individuals have picked up on these activities through horizontal transmission? Is a woman with a severe learning disability who is in terror of nearly all the scenes in *The Wizard of Oz*, and can relate them to tortures not mentioned in the film, a victim of mind control as well as ritual abuse? What happened to all the prominent scientists proven to have been involved in creating DID? What ideas and practices did they pass on to the next generation? It is too soon to be able to give a clear answer, but if we do not look at the official documentation that is already available (Ross, 2006), we will be less able to help those who come to us for help.

Links have been made with Freemasonry and every religion, old and new. Alistair Crowley was a 33rd Degree Freemason, the highest level, and Lieutenant Romola had a Level 33 inside. An interest in holy numbers and numerology is also found in Islam and the Kabala, and we have found that people come to us from all religious or quasi-religious backgrounds. As with child abuse in the 1980s, we slowly realized that it was possible from all social and religious backgrounds. This is also true with mind control and mind control linked with a belief system.

While the actions of governments, religious bodies, institutions, families, and individuals might surface years later, and documentation might be found for some, for many crimes the key evidence is the mind and body of the victim. When we see ripples in a deep pond we know something has been thrown in it, even though we cannot properly discern what the object was. The men, women, and children who come with the distress of fragmented minds and memories are living evidence of hurt, even where we cannot find who or what shattered them.

The importance of love and positive attachments

Lieutenant Romola settled in the United Kingdom and is now married with two loved children. More important than anything else, love and positive attachments are the keys for any hope and change. Some programs can never be changed. Some people will remain in a mental prison, however, within the prison-house of the human body and mind, the warmth and light that love provides can still find a way.

CHAPTER FIFTEEN

Mind control: simple to complex

Ellen P. Lacter

Organizations with a wide range of political and criminal agendas have historically relied on coercive interrogation and brainwashing of various types to force submission and information from enemies and victims, and to indoctrinate and increase cooperation in members and captors. In modern times, these techniques are used by political, military, and espionage organizations, race and ethnic hate-groups, criminal groups (e.g. child pornographers and sex rings, and international traffickers of women, children, guns, and drugs), and exploitative and destructive cults with spiritual, political, and/or financial agendas. Methods of thought reform used by such groups include intimidation, deception, shaming, social isolation, religious indoctrination, threats against victims or their loved ones, torture, torture of co-captives, and brainwashing through social influence, regimentation of activities, or deprivation of basic needs, such as sleep or food (Hassan, 2000).

Mental health and law-enforcement professionals working with severe trauma are increasingly seeing victims of torture administered with the purpose of installation of more covert mind

control—that is, mind control that was installed in a deeply dissociated (without conscious awareness) state and that controls the
person from these unconscious, dissociated states of mind (Boyd,
1991; Coleman, 1994; Hersha, Hersha, Griffis, & Schwarz, 2001;
Katchen & Sakheim, 1992; Keith, 1997; Marks, 1979; Neswald &
Gould, 1993; Neswald, Gould, & Graham-Costain, 1991; Noblitt
& Perskin, 2000; Oksana, 2001; Ross, 2000; Rutz, 2001; Ryder &
Noland, 1992; Scheflin & Opton, 1978; M. Smith, 1993; Weinstein,
1990). The evidence of the existence of covert mind control has
begun to surface in the legal arena as well (e.g. *Orlikow v. U.S.*, 682
F.S. 77 [D.D.C. 1988]).

I shall outline various forms of mind control, beginning with
thought reform that is registered consciously, with memory, then
moving on to the most covert forms of mind control, in which the
individual has no memory of the installation and is controlled
beyond conscious awareness.

*Levels of brainwashing and mind control,
from the least to the most complex and binding*

At the most basic level, terrified submission is used to control
behaviour. The individual outwardly complies with the abuser(s),
but the individual's own beliefs and identity are consciously pre-
served.

In other cases, an individual may be induced to comply willingly. For example, a troubled or abused person is provided with
objects, drugs, affection, sex, "freedom", and so forth and consciously chooses compliance with the abuser over his/her current
life situation.

In cases of religious indoctrination, a psychologically weak or
dependent person submits to a charismatic leader who professes
to be chosen for a spiritual agenda by a powerful deity, and who
promises salvation to devotees and eternal damnation to non-
followers.

Cases of "Stockholm syndrome" involve deeper psychological controls. Terrorization (harm or threats of harm to the victim
and/or victim's loved ones), plus isolation from prior support,
often combined with lies of abandonment by loved ones, lead

to dependence on the abuser(s) and perceived loyalty to the abuser(s).

The term "brainwashing" is typically used to describe the use of a combination of social influence, regimentation of routine, and deprivation of basic needs, to attain still-fuller control of the individual's mind. A person is placed only among successful "converts" to the abuser or group, who profess the belief system of the group, while the person is isolated from loved ones and previous support systems and activities. Basic needs, including sleep, food, and water, are withdrawn, and activities are regimented to modify beliefs, including chanting, praying, indoctrination, and social isolation.

At a more sophisticated level, modification of self-view as evil or as an accomplice to a crime is used. Abusers may force an individual into double-binds to cause the individual to feel morally culpable. The individual is told to make a choice to commit a morally reprehensible act, such as hurting a person or animal, with an implied or direct threat that unbearable harm will come to self or others for failure to "choose" this act.

Another form of mind control is spiritual in nature, resulting in the perception of evil and threatening attachments, claims, curses, and covenants. In abusive rituals, witchcraft (not Wicca) abusers seek to attach evil entities (spirits of abusers and demons) to dissociated identities to harass and control victims for their entire lives. Abusive claims are used to forever malevolently define victims as evil, physically or mentally ill, socially devalued and isolated, sexually enslaved, a murderer, a cult member, a witch, and so forth. Curses, hexes, vexes, and spells are used to attempt to inflict physical and psychological harm. Witchcraft covenants are perceived agreements, generally made in reaction to terrorization or double-binds, to cause the victim to believe he or she freely committed to the abusers' agenda.

A further method of mind control is "psychic driving", in which taped messages are played non-stop for hours while the person is in states of consciousness altered by electroshock, drugs, isolation, confinement, deprivation of sleep, food, water, sleep, oxygen, and sensory input, or other torture. This methodology was utilized by Dr Ewen Cameron in the 1950s. In 1997, the CIA was sued by a number of Cameron's ex-patients. The Canadian court found in favour of the patients who endured Cameron's tortures in the name of creating a more efficient Manchurian Candidate for the CIA. Ross (2000) and Rutz (2001) also describe the US CIA projects—MKULTRA and others—which used unwitting human subjects for mind-control experimentation and exploitation.

Still more sophisticated abusers give commands to dissociated ego-states. Abusers administer torture, often combined with drugs, to obstruct the individual's conscious processing and to access dissociated ego-states (identities, personalities) formed in earlier abuse. The designated personalities are commanded to commit acts or to think and fear particular things that further the abusers' agenda. Common mandates include, "Remember to forget" the abuse, and "Don't tell" about the abuse. In child victims who do not yet have any dissociated identities, torture may be applied to force the formation of a new ego-state who can thereafter be manipulated to serve the abuser's agenda. In individuals with already-formed dissociated ego-states, as in dissociative identity disorder, a particular method of torture may be used to access a particular ego-state of whom the abuser has prior knowledge. Alternatively, a new form of torture may be applied to force the psyche to create a new ego-state, whom the abusers will then use for a new purpose. A central function of this technique is to cause the victim to re-experience, both physically and psychologically, the pain and terror of the tortured ego-states should the individual consider violating abuser commands. The experience of the original torture often leaks to the host personality in rushes of terror and somatic manifestations of the abuse, such as pain, bruising, or swelling (though not to the degree of the original injury), with no conscious registration of the abuse or abused ego-state.

Trauma-based mind-control programming

Trauma-based mind-control programming further exploits dissociated ego states to more efficiently control the individual on a deeply unconscious level. Systematic torture is used to block the victim's capacity for conscious processing (through pain, terror, drugs, illusion, hypnosis, sensory deprivation, sensory overstimulation, oxygen deprivation, cold, heat, spinning, brain stimulation, etc., and often, near-death), followed by the use of suggestion and/or classical and operant conditioning (consistent with well-established behaviour-modification principles) to implant thoughts, directives, and perceptions in the unconscious mind, often in newly formed trauma-induced dissociated identities, that force the victim to do, feel, think, or perceive things for the purposes of the programmer. The objective is for the victim to follow directives with no conscious awareness, including execution of acts in clear violation of the victim's moral principles, spiritual convictions, and volition.

Installation of mind-control programming relies on the victim's capacity to form new dissociated ego-states (personalities) to hold and hide programming behind walled-off amnesic barriers. Already dissociative children are prime candidates for programming. Alternatively, very young children can be made to be dissociative through torture. The extreme abuse inflicted on young children in familial satanic and witchcraft cults intentionally and reliably induces the formation of dissociated ego-states in the psyche. Many ritual abuse survivors report that other abuser groups with criminal, political, military, and espionage agendas infiltrate their familial cults to gain access to these readily programmable children to use them to serve their own agendas, often paying cult parents large sums of money to be able to program these children.

One common function of trauma-based mind-control programming is to cause the victim to physically and psychologically re-experience the torture used to install the programming should the victim consider violating its directives. The most common programs are unidimensional directives communicated during torture and impaired states of consciousness to "Remember to forget" the abuse and "Don't tell" about the abuse.

Much trauma-based mind-control programming is significantly more complex, more technological in its methods of installation, and utilizes the individual's dissociated ego-states (personalities) to effect greater layering of psychological effects. Personalities are usually programmed to take executive control of the mind and body in response to particular cues (hand signals, tones, spoken names, etc.), and then follow directives, with complete amnesia for these events. Personalities are programmed to become flooded with anxiety or feel acutely suicidal if they defy program directives. Personalities are often programmed to believe that explosives, toxins, and so forth have been surgically implanted in their bodies and that these will detonate or release if the individual violates orders or begins to recall the programming, the torture used to install it, or the identities of the programmers. Many mind-control survivors eventually recall a staged surgery to make them believe a device was installed to harm or monitor them. The illusion usually includes people dressed in white coats, and superficial cuts and stitches.

In highly sophisticated mind control, the individual is programmed to perceive structures in the unconscious inner landscape. "Structures" are mental representations of objects—for example, buildings, grids, devices of torture, and other containers—that hold programmed commands, messages, information, and personalities. In many cases, walls are also installed that serve as barriers to hide deeper levels of programming and structures. Unconscious personalities perceive themselves as trapped within, or attached to, these structures, both visually (in internal imagery) and somatically (in experiences of pain, suffocation, electroshock, etc.).

Structures are installed in early childhood, generally between 2 and 5 years of age. Torture and drugs are applied beyond the endurance of all of the already formed personalities, which usually requires that the child be taken near death. The intent is to bury all memory for the event deeply in the unconscious mind, below the level of conscious perception of all personalities. When all conscious processing of information is blocked, the child cannot mentally process or mentally resist any of the programmer's input, cannot reject it as "not me" or as untrue. Instead, the input is "taken in whole", into the unconscious mind, with no conscious memory, and therefore no ability to recall, process, or reject it later.

The child may be tortured on or in a device, and the personalities formed in this process then perceive themselves trapped on or in this device. Alternatively, an image of an object may be projected on the child's body or on a screen or in virtual-reality goggles, or a physical model of the object may be shown. The programmer then tells the child that this device or object is now within him or her. Because the mind of the small child does not easily discriminate reality from fantasy (this process relies, in part, on the pre-school child's stage of magical thinking), the child now perceives the object as a structure within.

Immediately after the structure is installed, the programmer will generally command traumatized personalities to go to places in the structures—for example, "Go inside the grid." The programmer will generally also install the perception of wires, bombs, and reset buttons, to prevent removal of the structure. The child is usually shown something to make him or her perceive these as real—for example, wires placed on body parts and a button on the belly-button.

Program triggers, cues, and access codes are also installed, to gain future access to the structure and to programmed personalities. This permits the programmer to install, change, and erase commands, messages, and information and to retrieve information, all out of victims' conscious awareness. An erase code for the structure is also installed to allow the programmer to later erase a defective, outdated, or unwanted structure. I have witnessed survivors from distant geographical areas report the identical erase code for the same structure.

Personalities trapped in or on structures generally obey program directives until psychologically released from the structures. Programmed functions are usually performed unconsciously, or the victim may experience a strong, terror-driven compulsion to do, or not do, something. For example, personalities are often programmed to awaken at an early morning hour to make a telephone call (the abusers' use of toll-free numbers results in no record of these calls) to obtain or provide information to an abuser group. Programmed "reporter" personalities report whether therapy is approaching the hidden programming. The host personality usually has no knowledge of making these calls or may awaken to find him/herself holding a telephone in the middle of the night, not knowing why. Some survivors of programming become aware of compulsions to perform particular acts and learn to recognize these as "not me"—as programming—and to override them.

Effects of complex mind control

Complex mind control is designed to override a victim's free will, to force victims to follow commands and perform actions that are in clear violation of their moral principles and spiritual convictions, generally without conscious awareness. These kinds of programming tend to exert control over the individual for decades, often with no conscious awareness of the programming or of the personalities under its control. Survivors of severe abuse, especially of ritual abuse, often begin to recover their memories between 30 and 50 years of age. It may be many years more before a person becomes aware of sophisticated mind-control programming and its ongoing effects on her or him. For example, some survivors recall an abusive satanic or witchcraft ritual but experience a blank spot in the middle of the memory. This missing piece is discovered years later to be the part of the ritual involving sophisticated trauma-based mind control.

Some common indicators of trauma-based mind-control programming

Most survivors of programming will have many of the indicators of trauma-based mind-control programming outlined below. However, the presence of indicators does not prove the existence of programming trauma. Conversely, their absence does not mean that a person has no such trauma. The more successful the programming, the more symptom-free the individual.

The person may experience suicidal and self-harm impulses and/or thoughts that do not feel like they originate in their true feelings or wishes, but instead feel relatively unconnected to the self. They may have a perception of inanimate, mechanistic, mathematical, or laboratory-like objects in the mind or elsewhere in the body. Or they may make repetitive, robotic statements that do not make sense in the context of a dialogue—for example, "I want to go home" (generally meaning to return to the abuser group). These individuals may have obsessive, robotic thoughts—for example, irrelevant alpha-numeric series running through their mind, or singing the same song. Some may display compulsive or ritualized behaviours—for example, odd hand-movements. They may self-mutilate, particularly in pictures or patterns. The person may display a pattern of suddenly leaving home for the evening or weekend, or longer, to a motel or park, and so forth. He or she may create a conflict with loved ones, which is understood later as having been driven by the need to leave the home. Such an indicator is of greater weight if these sudden trips occur yearly at the same times, or if the individual has no continuous memory for how he or she spent the time away.

The person may dread his or her own birthday, Christmas, Easter, or other days, without conscious memory of a frightening event on that date. There may be increased depression, anxiety, self-harm, or suicidality on holidays, birthdays, equinoxes, solstices, and so forth. The individual may have large gaps in memory, often for an entire year or more of their childhood, with greater recall for times before and immediately after that period of time. There may be no memory for particular past places of residence. The person may display unusual behaviour in relation to the telephone—for example, strong fear or a startle response to the phone ringing, many hang-up calls coming to the home, a compulsion to make calls (often toll-free), or finding the phone in his or her hands in the early morning hours without any memory of having made a phone call. There may be a pattern of increased "dead-air" phone calls in which no one answers when they pick up the phone and say "Hello", particularly on cult call-back dates, such as birthdays or ritual holidays.

They may have a great sensitivity to indoor lights, often needing bright lights to be turned off or dimmed. The person may have fear responses to water: he or she may not be able to drink it, or rain may feel as if it is burning hot or like acid, or he or she may have a fear of bathing, or difficulty taking showers. There may be fear responses to benign stimuli—for example, mirrors (very common), colours (common), shapes (common), food brands, animals, hearing one's name called, cartoon characters, and so on. They may have unexplained behavioural compulsions, such as a strongly felt need to eat or drink a particular thing, go to a particular place, or perform a particular act. Common fears and phobias include watching-eyes, detached faces and heads, severed limbs, monsters or demons, snakes, spiders, rats, coffins, dark holes, cages, baths, drowning, being buried, swords, knives, and guns. These objects also often appear in art productions, sand trays (sandplay therapy), poetry, and dreams.

Progress in psychotherapy or memory recovery may result in increased suicidality, self-harm (burns, drug overdose, cuts), depression, anxiety, cancelled psychotherapy sessions, or urges to stop therapy. During therapy sessions, they may experience sleepiness, lost time, feeling stuck, a feeling of having been "called away" for most of session, or an inability to speak to the therapist or hear the therapist. They may experience severe flinching and spasms, as if being electroshocked, when approaching trauma material. Memories of trauma are regularly followed by a denying statement, such as, "I must have made it all up".

Removal of programming

Discovering carefully hidden programming, and personalities perceiving themselves inexorably trapped in programming, generally requires a means of safely accessing information stored in the unconscious mind. Programmers go to great lengths to sabotage any attempt to discover or disable their programs, by installing self-destruction programs and physical and psychological consequences that are intended to be set off should anyone approach the programming. The host may be determined to defy such consequences, but programmed personalities are likely to perceive themselves as stuck in the sites of their abuse, and their fear, terror, pain, and somatic reactions tend to leak through to the host. Finding, disabling, and removing programming must skilfully sidestep these programmed negative consequences. The process also requires vigilance for red herrings—decoys installed by abusers, and smoke screens put up by frightened personalities.

The objective of program removal is to remove the perception of all injunctions and implants (structures, hostile spiritual controls, etc.), and to free all personalities controlled by programming, so they may act of their own free will to decide who and what they want to be and do. The free will of the host and other personalities must be respected at all times in the process of disabling mind-control programming. Program removal cannot be achieved with re-programming or abuse—for example, use of coercion, manipulation, deceit, intimidation, or sleep deprivation. Once released from program controls, affected personalities can leave the sites of their trauma and program structures, go to a healing or safe place in the inner world, and/or gain co-consciousness with the host or integrate with the host. In many cases, this process enables the host to integrate with a hidden "core", a significant and central aspect of the self that the individual had long kept hidden from abusers.

REFERENCES

APA (2000). *Diagnostic and Statistical Manual of Mental Disorders* (4th edition, Text Revision). Washington, DC: American Psychiatric Association.

Appelbaum, P. S., & Gutheil, T. G. (2007). *Clinical Handbook of Psychiatry and the Law* (4th edition). Philadelphia, PA: Wolters Kluwer/ Lippincott Williams & Wilkins.

Arendt, H. (1963). *Eichmann in Jerusalem: A Report on the Banality of Evil.* London: Faber.

Bion, W. R. (1967). A theory of thinking. In: *Second Thoughts.* London: Karnac.

Blass, T. (2002). Perpetrator behavior as destructive obedience: An evaluation of Stanley Milgram's perspective, the most influential social-psychological approach to the Holocaust. In L. S. Newman & R. Erber (Eds.), *Understanding Genocide: The Social Psychology of the Holocaust.* Oxford: Oxford University Press.

Blass, T. (2004). *The Man Who Shocked the World: The Life and Legacy of Stanley Milgram.* New York: Basic Books.

Bowart, W. (1977). *Operation Mind Control.* New York: Dell.

Bowlby, J. (1958). The nature of the child's tie to his mother. *International Journal of Psychoanalysis, 39*: 350–373.

Bowlby, J. (1969). *Attachment and Loss, Vol. 1: Attachment.* London: Hogarth Press & The Institute of Psychoanalysis.

Bowlby, J. (1973). *Attachment and Loss, Vol. 2: Separation, Anxiety and Anger.* London: Hogarth Press & The Institute of Psychoanalysis.

Bowlby, J. (1988). On knowing what you are not supposed to know and feeling what you are not supposed to feel. In: *A Secure Base: Clinical Applications of Attachment Theory* (pp. 99–118). London: Routledge.

Boyd, A. (1991). *Blasphemous Rumours: Is Satanic Ritual Abuse Fact or Fantasy? An Investigation.* London: HarperCollins.

Brandon, S., Boakes, J., Glaser, D., & Green, R. (1998). Recovered memories of childhood sexual abuse: Implications for clinical practice. *British Journal of Psychiatry, 172:* 296–307.

British Psychological Society (1995). *Recovered Memories. The Report of the Working Party of the British Psychological Society.* Leicester: Author.

Cameron, D. E. (1956). Psychic driving. *American Journal of Psychiatry, 112:* 502–509.

Coleman, J. (1994). Satanic cult practices. In: V. Sinason (Ed.), *Treating Survivors of Satanist Abuse* (pp. 242–253). London: Routledge.

Davies, J., & Frawley, M. (1994). *Treating the Adult Survivor of Childhood Sexual Abuse: A Psychoanalytic Perspective.* New York: Basic Books.

Delgado, J. M. R. (1971). *Physical Control of the Mind: Toward a Psychocivilized Society.* New York: Harper & Row.

Dell, P. F. (2002). Dissociative phenomenology of dissociative identity disorder. *Journal of Nervous and Mental Diseases, 190:* 10–15.

Dell, P. F. (2006). A new model of dissociative identity disorder. *Psychiatric Clinics of North America, 29:* 1–26.

deMause, L. (1974). *The History of Childhood.* New York: Psychohistory Press.

Estabrooks, G. H. (1971). Hypnosis comes of age. *Science Digest* (April): 44–50.

Fink, D. L. (1988). The core self: A developmental perspective on the dissociative disorders. *Dissociation, 1:* 43–47.

Frankel, S., & Roseman, M. E. (1999). Dissociation and the law. *International Society for the Study of Dissociation News, 16* (March): 3.

Fröhling, U. (1996). *Vater unser in der Hoelle* ["Our Father in Hell"] (revised edition). Bergisch-Gladbach: Bastei, 2008.

Garland, C. (Ed.) (2002). *Understanding Trauma: A Psychoanalytical Approach* (revised edition). London: Karnac.

Great Britain, Dept. of Health (1994). *The Extent and Nature of Organised and Ritual Abuse. Research Findings.* Report by J. S. La Fontaine. London: HMSO.

Green, A. (1986). The dead mother. In: *On Private Madness*. London: Hogarth Press.

Grotstein, J. (1981). *Splitting and Projective Identification*. New York: Jason Aronson.

Hale, R., & Sinason, V. (1994). Internal and external reality: Establishing parameters. In V. Sinason (Ed.), *Treating Survivors of Satanist Abuse* (pp. 274–284). London: Routledge.

Hammond, D. C. (1992). "Hypnosis in MPD: Ritual Abuse" [usually known as "The Greenbaum Speech"]. Talk given at the Fourth Annual Eastern Regional Conference on Abuse and Multiple Personality, Alexandria, VA, 25 June.

Hassan, S. (2000). *Releasing the Bonds: Empowering People to Think for Themselves.* Danbury, CT: Aitan Publishing.

Hersha, L., Hersha, C., Griffis, D., & Schwarz, T. (2001). *Secret Weapons: Two Sisters' Terrifying True Story of Sex, Spies, and Sabotage.* Far Hills, NJ: New Horizon Press.

Hesse, E. (1996). Discourse, memory, and the Adult Attachment Interview: A note with emphasis on the emerging Cannot Classify category. *Infant Mental Health Journal, 17*: 4–11.

Hesse, E., & Main, M. (2000). Disorganized infant, child, and adult attachment: Collapse in behavioral and attention strategies. *Journal of the American Psychoanalytic Association, 48*: 1097–1127.

Hollins, S., & Sinason, V. (2000). Psychotherapy, learning disabilities and trauma: New perspectives. *British Journal of Psychiatry, 176*: 32–36.

Icke, D. (2002). *Alice in Wonderland and the World Trade Center Disaster: Why the Official Story of 9/11 Is a Monumental Lie.* Wildwood, MO: Bridge of Love.

Kahr, B. (1994). Multiple personality disorder and schizophrenia: An interview with Professor Flora Rheta Schreiber. In V. Sinason (Ed.), *Attachment, Trauma and Multiplicity.* Hove: Brunner-Routledge, 2002.

Kahr, B. (2007). Infanticidal attachment. *Attachment: New Directions in Psychotherapy and Relational Psychoanalysis, 1*: 117–132.

Karriker, W. (2007). "Helpful Healing Methods: As Rated by Approximately 900 Respondents to the EAS." Paper presented at the meeting of the International Society for the Study of Trauma and Dissociation, Philadelphia, PA.

Katchen, M., & Sakheim, D. (1992). Satanic beliefs and practices. In: D. K. Sakheim & S. F. Devine (Eds.), *Out of Darkness: Exploring Satanism and Ritual Abuse* (pp. 21–43). New York: Lexington Books.

Keith, J. (1997). *Mind Control, World Control*. Kempton, IL: Adventures Unlimited Press.

Kernberg, O. (1975). *Borderline Conditions and Pathological Narcissism*. New York: Jason Aronson.

Klein, M. (1946). Notes on some schizoid mechanisms. In: *Envy and Gratitude and Other Works 1946–1963* (pp. 292–320). London: Hogarth Press, 1975.

Laub, D., & Auerhahn N. C. (1993). Knowing and not knowing massive psychic trauma: Forms of traumatic memory. *International Journal of Psychoanalysis*, 74: 287–302.

Levy, S., & Lemma, A. (2004). *The Perversion of Loss: Psychoanalytic Perspectives on Trauma*. London: Whurr.

Lidz, T. (1973). *The Origin and Treatment of Schizophrenic Disorders*. New York: Basic Books.

Lifton, R. J. (1986). *The Nazi Doctors: Medical Killing and the Psychology of Genocide*. New York: Basic Books.

Lifton, R. J. (2000). *Destroying the World to Save It: Aum Shinrikyo, Apocalyptic Violence, and the New Global Terrorism*. New York: Owl Books.

Liotti, G. (1999). Understanding the dissociative processes: The contribution of attachment theory. *Psychoanalytic Inquiry*, 19: 757–783.

Liotti, G. (2006). A model of dissociation based on attachment theory and research. *Journal of Trauma and Association*, 7: 55–74.

Louisiana Statutes (1989). *Statute #107.1: Ritualistic Acts.* Retrieved January 18, 2008, from http://dissoc.de/louisiana.html

Lowenstein, R. J. (1991). An office mental status examination for complex chronic dissociative symptoms and multiple personality disorder. *Psychiatric Clinics of North America*, 14: 567–604.

Marks, J. (1979). *The Search for the Manchurian Candidate: The CIA and Mind Control*. New York: Times Books.

Middleton, W. (2005). Owning the past, claiming the present: Perspectives on the treatment of dissociative patients. *Australasian Psychiatry, 13*: 40–49.

Middleton, W., & Butler, J. (1998). Dissociative identity disorder: An Australian series. *Australian and New Zealand Journal of Psychiatry, 32*: 794–804.

Milgram, S. (1963). Behavioral study of obedience. *Journal of Abnormal and Social Psychology, 67*: 371–378.

Milgram, S. (1974). *Obedience to Authority: An Experimental View*. London: Tavistock.

Miller, A. (1980). *For Your Own Good: Hidden Cruelty in Child-Rearing and the Roots of Violence*, transl. H. & H. Hannum. London: Faber & Faber, 1983. [Published in German as *Am Anfang war Erziehung*. Frankfurt: Suhrkamp Verlag.]

Mollon, P. (1996). *Multiple Selves, Multiple Voices: Working with Trauma, Violation and Dissociation*. Chichester: Wiley.

Mollon, P. (1998). *Remembering Trauma: A Psychotherapist's Guide to Memory and Illusion*. Chichester: Wiley.

Mollon, P. (2002a). *Remembering Trauma: A Psychotherapist's Guide to Memory and Illusion* (2nd edition). London: Whurr.

Mollon, P. (2002b). Dark dimensions of multiple personality. In: V. Sinason (Ed.) *Attachment, Trauma, and Multiplicity* (pp. 177–194). Hove: Brunner-Routledge.

Neswald, D., & Gould, C. (1993). Basic treatment and program neutralization strategies for adult MPD survivors of satanic ritual abuse. *Treating Abuse Today, 4* (3): 14–19.

Neswald, D., Gould, C., & Graham-Costain, V. (1991). "Common programs" observed in survivors of satanic ritual abuse. *The California Therapist, 3* (5): 47–50.

Noblitt, J. R., & Perskin, P. (2000). *Cult and Ritual Abuse: Its History, Anthropology and Recent Discovery in Contemporary America* (revised edition). Westport, CT: Praeger.

Oksana, C. (2001). *Safe Passage to Healing: A Guide for Survivors of Ritual Abuse* (revised edition). New York: Harper Perennial.

Phillips, M., & O'Brien, C. (1995). *Trance Formation of America: The True Life Story of a CIA Mind Control Slave*. Las Vegas, NV: Reality Marketing.

Putnam, F. W. (1989). *Diagnosis and Treatment of Multiple Personality Disorder*. New York: Guilford Press.

Putnam, F. W. (1997). *Dissociation in Children and Adolescents: A Developmental Perspective*. New York: Guilford Press.

Putnam, F. W., & Trickett, P. K. (1993). "Dissociation and the Development of Psychopathology." Paper presented at symposium on The Development of Maltreated Children, Annual Meeting of the Society for Research in Child Development, New Orleans, March.

Ross, C. A. (2000). *BLUEBIRD: Deliberate Creation of Multiple Personality by Psychiatrists*. Richardson, TX: Manitou Communications.

Ross, C. A. (2004). *Schizophrenia: Innovations in Diagnosis and Treatment*. New York: Hawarth Press.

Ross, C. A. (2006). *The CIA Doctors: Human Rights Violations by American Psychiatrists*. Richardson, TX: Manitou Communications.

Rutz, C. (2001). *A Nation Betrayed: The Chilling True Story of Secret Cold War Experiments Performed on Our Children and Other Innocent People*. Grass Lake, MI: Fidelity Publishing.

Rutz, C. (2003). *Carul Rutz's Lecture at Indiana University in November 2003*. Retrieved January 18, 2008, from http://my.dmci.net/~casey/Indiana%20University%20Lecture%202003.html

Rutz, C., & Karriker, W. (2008). *Government-Funded Mind Control/Medical Experimentation (Quotes to Ponder)*. Retrieved January 18, 2008, from http://my.dmci.net/~casey/mcadvocacyre.3.pdf

Ryder, D., & Noland, J. T. (1992). *Breaking the Circle of Satanic Ritual Abuse: Recognizing and Recovering from the Hidden Trauma*. Minneapolis, MN: CompCare.

Sachs, A. (1997). Attachment: A matter of life and death. In: *Invisible Violence: On the Mechanism of Intergenerational Transmission of Massive Trauma*. Unpublished dissertation, City University, London.

Saks, E. (2001). Multiple personality disorder and criminal responsibility. *Southern California Interdisciplinary Law Journal*, 10: 179–203.

Sandler, J., & Fonagy, P. (Eds.) (1997). *Recovered Memories of Abuse: True or False?* London: Karnac.

Scheflin, A. W. (2003). Dissociation and the law: Is MPD/DID a defense to crime? Part II. *International Society for the Study of Dissociation News*, 21: 2–4, 12.

Scheflin, A. W., & Opton, E. (1978). *The Mind Manipulators*. New York: Grosset & Dunlap.

Schopp, R. F. (2001). Multiple personality disorder, accountable agency, and criminal acts. *Southern California Interdisciplinary Law Journal*, 10: 297–334.

Schore, A. (1994). *Affect Regulation and the Origin of the Self: The Neurobiology of Emotional Development*. Hillsdale, NJ: Laurence Erlbaum Associates.

Schore, A. (2003). *Affect Dysregulation and Disorders of the Self*. New York: Norton.

Sinason, V. (Ed.) (1994). *Treating Survivors of Satanist Abuse*. London: Routledge.

Sinason, V. (Ed.) (1998). *Memory in Dispute*. London: Karnac.

Sinason, V. (Ed.) (2002). *Attachment, Trauma and Multiplicity: Working with Dissociative Identity Disorder*. Hove: Routledge.

Sinnott-Armstrong, W., & Behnke, S. (2001). Criminal law and multiple personality disorder: The vexing problems of personhood and responsibility. *Southern California Interdisciplinary Law Journal, 10*: 277–296.

Smith, C. (2003). On the need for new criteria of diagnosis of psychosis in the light of mind invasive technology. *Journal of Psycho-Social Studies, 2* (2, No. 3). Retrieved January 27, 2008, from http://www.btinternet.com/~psycho_social/Vol3/JPSS-CS2.html

Smith, M. (1993). *Ritual Abuse: What It Is, Why It Happens, How To Help*. San Francisco, CA: Harper.

Southgate, J. (1996). "An Attachment Approach to Dissociation and Multiplicity." Paper presented at the Third John Bowlby Memorial Lecture, CAPP, London.

Southgate, J. (2002). A theoretical framework for understanding multiplicity and dissociation. In V. Sinason (Ed.), *Attachment, Trauma and Multiplicity: Working with Dissociative Identity Disorder* (pp. 86–106). Hove: Routledge.

Starrs, J. E. (2005). *A Voice for the Dead: A Forensic Investigator's Pursuit of the Truth in the Grave*. New York: Putnam.

Stern, D. N. (1985). *The Interpersonal World of the Infant: A View from Psychoanalysis and Developmental Psychology*. New York: Basic Books.

Thomas, G. (1989). *Journey into Madness: The True Story of Secret CIA Mind Control and Medical Abuse*. London: Bantam Books.

United Nations Commission on Human Rights (2002). *Contemporary Forms of Slavery—Report of the Working Group on Contemporary Forms of Slavery on its Twenty-Seventh Session*. Retrieved January 18, 2008, from http://www.unhchr.ch/Huridocda/Huridoca.nsf/e06a5300f90fa0238025668700518ca4/8ab7a0f2fbf0474ac1256c1000539eee/$FILE/G0214051.pdf van der Hart, O., Bolt, H., & van der Kolk, O. (2005). Memory fragmentation in dissociative identity disorder. *Journal of Trauma and Dissociation, 6*: 55–70.

van der Hart, O., & Nijenhuis, E. R. S. (1998). Recovered memories of abuse and dissociative identity disorder. *British Journal of Psychiatry, 173*: 537–538.

van der Hart, O., & Nijenhuis, E. R. S. (1999). Bearing witness to uncorroborated trauma: The clinician's development of reflective belief. *Professional Psychology: Research and Practice, 30*: 37–44.

van der Hart, O., Nijenhuis, E. R. S., & Steele, K. (2006). *The Haunted Self*. New York: Norton.

van der Kolk, B. A., McFarlane, A. C., & Weisaeth, L. (Ed.) (1996). *Traumatic Stress: The Effects of Overwhelming Stress on Mind, Body and Society*. New York: Guilford Press.

Vanier, A. (2000). *Lacan*. New York: Other Press.

Weinstein, H. M. (1990). *Psychiatry and the Central Intelligence Agency: Victims of Mind Control*. Washington, DC: American Psychiatric Press.

Wilkinson, M. (2006). *Coming into Mind. The Mind–Brain Relationship: A Jungian Clinical Perspective*. Hove: Brunner-Routledge.

Winnicott, D. W. (1965). *The Maturational Processes and the Facilitating Environment: Studies in the Theory of Emotional Development*. London: Hogarth Press & The Institute of Psycho-Analysis.

Winnicott, D. W. (1971). *Playing and Reality*. London: Tavistock.

INDEX

Freemasonry, 183
Fröhling, U., 38
Frye v United States, 89, 98
fugue state(s), 80
   psychogenic, 85

Galton, G., xvii, 4, 7, 116–126,
   140–144
Garland, C., 118
General Medical Council, 14
generational satanism, 20
"Geraldine" ["Aahbee"], 56
Germany, 35, 37, 38, 49
Glaser, D., 117
Gleeson [*Re: Gleeson*], 95, 98
Gnostic-occult group(s), 43, 44, 181
Gould, C., 186
government experimentation, 33,
   34
Graham-Costain, V., 186
Greece, 36, 37
Green, A., 132
Green, R., 117
"Green, Dr", 170–171, 174
Greene, W. B., 88, 89, 91, 92, 98
   Greene v Lambert, 92, 98
   State of Washington v Greene, 89,
      90, 92, 98
   "Tyrone", 89
Griffis, D., 186
Grimsley [*State of Ohio v Grimsley*],
   85, 86, 87, 90, 98
   "Jennifer", 85
   "Robin", 85
Grotstein, J., 109
Guantanamo Bay, 172
Gutheil, T. G., 93

"H" ["Louise"], 76, 77, 78
Hale, R., 120, 168
hallucination(s), 2, 5, 79, 97, 114
hallucinatory experiences, 113
hallucinatory voices, 80
Hammond, D. C., 174, 180
Hassan, S., 185
Healey, C., xvii, 3, 6, 23–31

Hersha, C., 186
Hersha, L., 186
Hesse, E., 129–131
Himmler, H., 174
historical truth, 7, 118
"HJ" ["Louise"], 62, 74–75, 76, 77,
   78
Hollins, S., 132, 139
Hong Kong, 36
"honour killings", 172
"host approach" to culpability, 92
Hungary, 37, 38
hypnosis/hypnotism, 20, 34, 95, 97,
   176, 182, 188
hypnotic access codes, 179
hysterical paralysis, 82

Icke, D., 179
identity:
   confusion, 80
   personal, 79, 176
   states, 80, 82, 84, 88, 95–97
ideologically motivated crimes
   (IMC), 32, 33, 39, 40, 48, 49
Illuminati, 180, 181
illusion(s), 161, 188, 190
imaginary vs real, 108–115
IMC (ideologically motivated
   crimes), 32, 33, 39, 40, 48, 49
incest, 11, 33, 34, 114
interrogation, coercive, 185
India, 36
indoctrination, 182, 185–187
infanticidal attachment, 7, 127–139
   concrete, 131–138
   symbolic, 131–138
infanticidal caregiver, 133
infanticidal ideation, 131, 133, 136,
   137
infanticide, 128
infantile phantasies, 109
infant trauma, 118, 119
injuries, personality-specific,
   149–150
insanity, 85, 89, 90, 92–94
   defence of, 87